Steve & Me

Steve & Me

Terri Irwin

Doubleday Large Print Home Library Edition

SIMON SPOTLIGHT ENTERTAINMENT
New York London Toronto Sydney

This Large Print Edition, prepared especially for Doubleday Large Print Home Library, contains the complete, unabridged text of the original Publisher's Edition.

SIMON SPOTLIGHT ENTERTAINMENT
An imprint of Simon & Schuster
1230 Avenue of the Americas,
New York, New York 10020

All insert photos are courtesy of the author's personal collection. The photo of Steve doing construction work, on page 6 of the photo insert, was taken by Graham Parkes. The photo of Steve and Terri with Harriet, on page 14 of the photo insert, was taken by Greg Barrett.

Manufactured in the United States of America

ISBN: 978-0-7394-8969-7

To our children, Bindi and Robert.
Keep these three things in your hearts:
faith, because it can move mountains;
hope, because it keeps you going
no matter what; and love, the greatest
of all. Love never dies.
Daddy and I will love you both forever.

Entreat me not to leave you
Or to return from following you;
For where you go I will go,
And where you lodge I will lodge;
Your people shall be my people,
And your God my God;
Where you die I will die,
And there will I be buried.
May the Lord do so to me
And more also
If even death parts me from you.

—Ruth 1:16

Contents

Foreword

I am extremely honored to be asked to write a few words about Steve, and it's only fitting that I was asked on Steve's research boat, *Croc One,* while conducting research on estuarine crocodiles with a team from Australia Zoo.

I am sitting near a campfire in a remote part of northern Australia as I write this. The campfire is an important ritual in my life that I look forward to every year when I visit here, but it is also a reminder of the man I am proud to call my friend, colleague, and mentor. In the early mornings as our campfire comes to life, I am transported back to the times Steve and I sat around the campfire and watched as the world we loved came to life. He talked of many things: his love for

Terri, Bindi, and Robert; his mum and dad; his plans for Australia Zoo; and championing wildlife conservation. But mostly, we talked about our one great shared love, crocodiles. We talked for hours about crocs, not only yarns of rogues and special animals but the quest for a greater understanding of these iconic animals. As the early-morning light rose over the campsite, we would tear ourselves away from our discussions and set out to conduct the research that would tell us even more about our icon.

A chance meeting with Steve about five years ago was the beginning of an exciting and amazing research partnership and friendship. Unbeknownst to many, Steve was a guiding force behind a research project monitoring the movements and behaviors of large crocodiles using cutting-edge satellite and acoustic telemetry. Steve brought to the research project his vast knowledge about crocodiles, his world-renowned expertise in catching them, his huge resources, and his passion to learn more about these remarkable animals. Steve was inspiring to work with, and he strongly believed that the more information he could find out about crocodiles and share with the world, the better we would understand, appreciate, and protect them.

While not formally trained as a researcher, he had many of the qualities a great scientist requires. He was driven by curiosity and had an endless list of questions. His thirst for knowledge was insatiable, and this was matched by his enthusiasm and desire to learn more. He was a brilliant man, with a great mind—a mind that continued to fascinate me with its ability to think of many things at once and retain amazing knowledge. His mind was expansive, it had no boundaries, and all of this was tempered by sensitivity and honesty, and richly colored by his passion. It is a gift when someone can challenge you and open your mind to new ideas. Steve did that for me, time and time again.

He was my teacher and my mentor in a field where I thought I had the jump on him. Little did I know the extent of his knowledge—his was truly gained by experience. As with the best teachers, he listened and learned from everyone around him in his quest for a greater understanding of not only crocodiles but all animals and the entire world around him. I was constantly surprised at how much he knew, at what scientific research he had read, and at his ability to communicate this knowledge in such an interesting and easy way.

In recognition of his standing and commitment to conservation and research, the University of Queensland was about to appoint him as an adjunct professor, an honor bestowed on only a few who have made a significant contribution to their field. Steve didn't know this had happened. The letter from the university arrived at Australia Zoo while we were in the field studying crocs during August 2006. He never got back to the pile of mail that included that letter. I know he would have proudly accepted the recognition of his achievement, but I also suspect that he would have remained humble and given credit to those around him, especially Terri, his mum and dad, Wes, John Stainton, and the incredible team at Australia Zoo.

A year later, in 2007, we are back here in northern Australia, continuing the research in his name. There is a big gap in all our lives, but I feel he is here, all around us. One sure sign is that the sixteen-foot crocodile we named "Steve" keeps turning up in our traps.

My life has been enriched by my friendship with Steve. I now sit around the fire with Terri, his family, and mates from Australia Zoo chatting about crocodiles and continuing the legacy Steve has left behind. Terri and Bob Irwin are now leading the croc-catching team from Australia Zoo, and Bindi is helping to affix the tracking devices to crocs, and so the tradition continues.

I miss him. We all do. But I can sit at the campfire and look into the coals and hear his voice, always intense, always passionate, telling us stories and goading us on to achieve more. The enthusiasm and determination Steve shared with us is alive and well.

He has touched so many lives. His memory will never fade, and this book will be one of the ways we can remind ourselves of our brush with the indomitable spirit of a loving husband, father, and son; a committed wildlife ambassador and conservationist; and a great mate.

Professor Craig E. Franklin, School of Integrative Biology
University of Queensland
Lakefield National Park
August 2007

CHAPTER ONE

First Encounter

The name of the zoo was the Queensland Reptile and Fauna Park. As I crossed the parking area, I prepared myself for disappointment. *I am going to see a collection of snakes, lizards, and miserable creatures in jars, feel terribly sorry for them, and leave.*

It was October 1991. I was Terri Raines, a twenty-seven-year-old Oregon girl in Australia on an unlikely quest to find homes for rescued American cougars. A reptile park wasn't going to be interested in a big cat. I headed through the pleasant spring heat toward the park thinking pessimistic thoughts. *This is going to be a big waste of time.* But the prospect of seeing new species of wildlife drew me in.

I walked through the modest entrance

with some friends, only to be shocked at what I found on the other side: the most beautiful, immaculately kept gardens I had ever encountered. Peacocks strutted around, kangaroos and wallabies roamed freely, and palm trees lined all the walkways. It was like a little piece of Eden.

After I paid my admission fee, I saw that the reptile enclosures were kept perfectly clean—the snakes glistened. I kept rescued animals myself at home. I knew zoos, and I knew the variety of nightmares they can fall into. But I saw not a sign of external parasites on these animals, no old food rotting in the cages, no feces or shed skin left unattended.

So I enjoyed myself. I toured around, learned about the snakes, and fed the kangaroos. It was a brilliant, sunlit day.

"There will be a show at the crocodile enclosures in five minutes," a voice announced on the PA system. "Five minutes."

That sounded good to me.

I noticed the crocodiles before I noticed the man. There was a whole line of crocodilians: alligators, freshwater crocodiles, and one big saltie. Amazing, modern-day dinosaurs. I didn't know much about them, but I knew that they had existed unchanged for millions of years. They were a message from our past, from the dawn of time, among the most ancient creatures on the planet.

Then I saw the man. A tall, solid twentysomething (he appeared younger than he was, and had actually turned twenty-nine that February), dressed in a khaki shirt and shorts, barefoot, with blond flyaway hair underneath a big Akubra hat and a black-banded wristwatch on his left wrist. Even though he was big and muscular, there was something kind and approachable about him too.

I stood among the fifteen or twenty other park visitors and listened to him talk.

"They can live as long as or even longer than us," he said, walking casually past the big saltwater croc's pond. "They can hold their breath underwater for hours."

He approached the water's edge with a piece of meat. The crocodile lunged out of the water and snapped the meat from his hand. "This male croc is territorial," he explained, "and females become really aggressive when they lay eggs in a nest." He knelt beside the croc that had just tried to nail him. "Crocodiles are such good mothers."

Every inch of this man, every movement and word exuded his passion for the crocodilians he passed among. I couldn't help but notice that he never tried to big-note himself. He was there to make sure his audience admired the crocs, not himself.

I recognized his passion, because I felt some of it myself. I spoke the same way about cougars as this Australian zookeeper spoke about crocs. When I heard there would be a special guided tour of the Crocodile Environmental Park, I was first in line for a ticket. I had to hear more. This man was on fire with enthusiasm, and I felt I really connected with him, like I was meeting a kindred spirit.

What was the young zookeeper's name? Irwin. Steve Irwin.

Some of the topics Steve talked about that day were wonderful and new. I learned about the romantic life of crocodiles. There are courting rituals between males and females, and the male crocodiles are very gentle as they nudge up and down alongside the female, waiting until she is receptive. I'd never imagined that these dinosaur-like creatures could be loving, but he explained that they were quite passionate lovers and seemed to develop real affection for each other.

Affection for each other, sure, but not for Steve. I watched the still, dark, murky water erupt with an enormous ton of saltwater crocodile. The croc nearly snapped the buttons off of Steve's shirt as he neatly deposited a piece of meat into its mouth. The reverberation of the jaws coming back together sounded like a rifle report.

From where I stood on the other side of the fence, I could barely breathe. I didn't know how he did it.

Other topics were more familiar. "Sometimes just seeing a croc in the wild can scare the daylights out of people," he said, passing among the rows of subadult crocodiles. "But if you know to follow some simple rules, these little tackers pose no threat at all to human life."

It was a situation that I'd encountered many times in the United States with predatory animals. People would frequent a boat ramp, for example. They'd come in with their catch and fillet it right at the dock, tossing the fish bones and scraps into the water. In the States, this might attract black bears, posing a potential problem for tourists. In Australia, the same practice brought the crocs into contact with humans.

"If we get a report about a particularly naughty little crocodile bothering people," Steve explained, "I go out with my dog, Sui, in a dinghy. We'll capture the croc so it won't get shot."

Then he described what he meant by "capture." As he told the story I was totally captivated, and so were the other zoo visitors. Maybe it was because Steve was detailing the most astonishing set of actions any of us had ever heard about, accomplished by a man who'd lived to tell the tale.

"If the croc is young, six feet long or smaller," he said, "I'll catch it by hand."

By hand. I'd had to capture all kinds of wildlife in Oregon, but never anything as dangerous as a six-foot-long saltwater crocodile . . . in the water . . . in the dark . . . by hand.

"We go out at night with a million-candle-power spotlight, shining bright across the water," he said. "That way, I can pick up the eye-shine of the crocodile. Their eyes glow bright red, right at the surface of the water. The croc thinks he's camouflaged by the darkness. He doesn't understand that my spotlight is revealing his location."

Idling the dinghy, bringing it quietly in closer and closer to the croc, Steve would finally make his move. He'd creep to the front of the boat and hold the spotlight until the last moment.

Then he would leap into the water.

Grabbing the crocodile around the scruff of the neck, he would secure its tail between his legs and wrap his body around the thrashing creature. Crocodiles are amazingly strong in the water. Even a six-foot-long subadult would easily take Steve to the bottom of the river, rolling and fighting, trying to dislodge him by scraping against the rocks and snags at the bottom of the river.

But Steve would hang on. He knew he could push off the bottom, reach the surface for air, flip the crocodile into his dinghy, and pin the snapping animal down.

"Piece of cake," he said.

That was the most incredible story I had ever heard. And Steve was the most incredible man I had ever seen—catching crocodiles by hand to save their lives? This was just unreal. I had an overwhelming sensation. I wanted to build a big campfire, sit down with Steve next to it, and hear his stories all night long. I didn't want them to ever end. But eventually the tour was over, and I felt I just had to talk to this man.

Steve had a broad, easy smile and the biggest hands I had ever seen. I could tell by his stature and stride that he was accustomed to hard work. I saw a series of small scars on the sides of his face and down his arms.

He came up and, with a broad Australian accent, said, "G'day, mate."

Uh-oh, I thought. *I'm in trouble.*

I'd never, ever believed in love at first sight. But I had the strangest, most overwhelming feeling that it was destiny that took me into that little wildlife park that day.

Steve started talking to me as if we'd known each other all our lives. I interrupted only to have my friend Lori take a picture of us, and the moment I first met Steve was forever captured. I told him about my wildlife rescue work with cougars in Oregon. He told me about his work with crocodiles.

The tour was long over, and the zoo was about to close, but we kept talking.

Finally I could hear Lori honking her horn in the car park. "I have to go," I said to Steve, managing a grim smile. I felt a connection as I never had before, and I was about to leave, never to see him again.

"Why do you love cougars so much?" he asked, walking me toward the park's front gate.

I had to think for a beat. There were many reasons. "I think it's how they can actually kill with their mouths," I finally said. "They can conquer an animal several times their size, grab it in their jaws, and kill it instantly by snapping its neck."

Steve grinned. I hadn't realized how similar we really were.

"That's what I love about crocodiles," he said. "They are the most powerful apex predators."

Apex predators. Meaning both cougars and crocs were at the top of the food chain. On opposite sides of the world, this man and I had somehow formed the same interest, the same passion.

At the zoo entrance I could see Lori and

her friends in the car, anxious to get going back to Brisbane.

"Call the zoo if you're ever here again," Steve said. "I'd really like to see you again." Could it be that he felt the same way I did? As we drove back to Brisbane, I was quiet, contemplative. I had no idea how I would accomplish it, but I was determined to figure out a way to see him. The next weekend, Lori was going diving with a friend, and I took a chance and called Steve.

"What do you reckon, could I come back for the weekend?" I asked.

"Absolutely. I'll take care of everything," came Steve's reply.

My heart was pounding as I drove up the coast again a few days later. There was the familiar little sign, the modest entrance. And here he was again, as large as life—six feet tall, broad shoulders, a big grin, and a warm and welcome handshake. Our first real touch.

"Well, I'm back," I said lamely.

"Good on you, mate," Steve said. I thought, *I've got what on me?*

Right away, I was extremely self-conscious about a hurdle I felt that we had to get over. I wasn't entirely sure about Steve's marital status. I looked for a ring, but he didn't wear one. *That doesn't mean anything,* I told myself. He probably can't wear one because of his work. I think he figured out what I was hinting at as I started asking him questions about his friends and family.

He lived right there at the zoo, he told me, with his parents and his sister Mandy. His sister Joy was married and had moved away.

I was trying to figure out how to say, "So, do you have a girlfriend?" when suddenly he volunteered the information.

"Would you like to meet my girlfriend?" he asked.

Ah, I felt my whole spirit sink into the ground. I was devastated. But I didn't want to show that to Steve.

I stood up straight and tall, smiled, and said, "Yes, I'd love to."

"Sue," he called out. "Hey, Sue."

Bounding around the corner came this little brindle girl, Sui, his dog.

"Here's me girlfriend," he said with a smile.

This is it, I thought. *There's no turning back.*

We spent a wonderful weekend together. I worked alongside him at the zoo from sunup to sunset. During the day it was raking the entire zoo, gathering up the leaves, cleaning up every last bit of kangaroo poo, washing out lizard enclosures, keeping the snakes clean. But it was the croc work that was most exciting.

The first afternoon of that visit, Steve took me in with the alligators. They came out of their ponds like sweet little puppies—puppies with big, sharp teeth and frog eyes. I didn't know what to expect, but with Steve there, I felt a sense of confidence and security. The next thing I knew, I was feeding the alligators big pieces of meat, as if I'd done it all my life.

That evening he put me up at the Glasshouse Mountains Motel, a few miles from the zoo. Steve was very chivalrous. I met his parents and had dinner with the whole family. I also got my first taste of Australian humor. That night at dinner, I poured myself what I thought was a nice glass of juice. The entire Irwin family sat quiet and straight-faced. As I took a big swig, it nearly choked me.

That's when I learned about cordial,

which is supposed to be mixed with water. I had poured it full strength. We all had a good laugh.

The next night Steve and I went to dinner in Caloundra, a nearby town. He took me to a resort that featured an all-you-can-eat buffet dinner—seafood banquet, my favorite. I loaded my plate high with prawns, crab, oysters, and everything I loved. I didn't know it then, but Steve was a bit worried that I was going to eat more than he did.

At one point a little piece of crab flicked onto the crook of my arm. I deftly reached down with my tongue and managed to grab it off my elbow and eat it. Suddenly I felt self-conscious. Steve was staring at me. He looked at me with such love in his eyes, and I thought, *He's going to say something wonderful.*

Steve leaned forward and said affectionately, "Gosh, you aren't ladylike at all." I burst out laughing. Apparently I'd done the right thing. I reflected back on my dad's advice: No matter what, always be yourself. And it sure had worked.

As we left the restaurant, Steve said, "You know, I smell ducks."

We walked outside, and sure enough, there was a flock of beautiful ducks bobbing around on a pond.

"Steve, you are the most amazing bushman I've ever met," I said.

Of course, the resort and the pond had been there for years, and Steve had known about the ducks for just as long. "I smell ducks" was a Crocodile Dundee trick that had nevertheless worked its magic on this naive American girl.

And then, suddenly, the weekend was over. Steve drove me back down to Brisbane. I had the biggest ache in my heart. I had fallen hard. As we said good-bye, he put his arms around me for the first time, and I felt all his strength and warmth in that embrace. But it was over. I was going back to my side of the world. I had no idea if I would ever see Steve Irwin again.

CHAPTER TWO

Malina

"Cougar cubs for sale."

Four words jumped out at me from the classified want ads in the *Oregonian,* a major newspaper in my home state of Oregon. It was 1986; I was twenty-two years old, living on my own, running a pilot car business I had inherited from my father.

I turned the page, closed the paper, and went on with my day. But those four words continued to thrum in my mind, and no matter what I did, I just couldn't seem to stop dwelling on them.

Cougar cubs, I thought. *That's strange. How can that be possible or legal when we've got cougars living in the wild in Oregon? How can you buy and sell them like pets?*

I tried to put the thought out of my mind, but I couldn't shake it. Finally I decided I had to drive up and check out the situation. The address was a residence in Hillsboro, a small suburb to the west of the city of Portland.

The owner of the place came out to meet me as I parked my car—he was a reed-thin smoker, with aviator glasses and thinning hair. He kept a lot of exotics on the grounds, a few parrots and monkeys, but mostly different and unusual breeds of horses, ranging in size from miniature ponies to big draft Percherons.

"I'm here to see the cougar cubs," I said.

"Only got one left," he told me, and led me back into a garage. A small portable pet carrier sat pushed up against one wall of the garage. I peered inside. A baby cougar stared blankly back out at me. She looked about three months old and was absolutely bone thin. Her eyes were dull and lifeless.

"Hello, sweetheart," I whispered. She barely looked up. She had tried so hard to get out of the cage that she had rubbed a large patch of fur off her forehead.

"What have you been feeding her?" I asked the owner. I detected the painful swelling of the joints that indicated rickets, the result of a poor or incorrect diet.

"Chicken necks," the owner said.

"Surely you've fed her something else as well?" I asked. The man shrugged and pushed his aviator glasses up on his nose.

"How much are you selling her for?"

"Thirteen hundred," he replied flatly.

Thirteen hundred dollars. A lot of money for me to come up with. I nodded thoughtfully, as if I were weighing the price.

"Well, thank you for showing her to me," I said.

I turned to leave, but I was so moved by that one little cougar that I knew I had to do something. I was a single woman living alone in a three-bedroom house in the suburbs. What on earth was I going to do with a baby cougar?

Eugene, Oregon, is the "Emerald City," beautifully situated at the end of the Willamette Valley. It's an outdoorsy, friendly kind of place, perfect for a soccer-playing, horse-riding, cheerleading young student at the Eugene Christian School, which is what I was. My mom, Julia, was a teacher. I was the baby of the family and the last child left at home. My sister Bonnie lived with us until I was six weeks old, when she moved out and got married. I knew my sister Tricia better, since she didn't get married until I was six. But for most of the time as I was growing up, I was well and truly entrenched as the only child.

My father, Clarence, worked a variety of jobs when I was growing up in Eugene. A heavy-haul trucker was one of them. He also ran the pilot cars that preceded and followed extra-wide loads on the highway. Because of his jobs on the road, he came across a lot of wounded or orphaned wildlife, and from time to time he'd come home with one. I was always keen to help any of these rescued creatures.

Driving his truck one day, my dad saw a mother merganser duck that had been hit by a car. Her baby ducks were with her, running around frantically back and forth at the side of the highway.

"Look," he said to me when he arrived at home that evening. He opened his jacket to reveal a half-dozen little ducklings. He couldn't stop with the big load when he first saw them, he said, but on the way back he managed to pull over and scoop up the few that he could find.

"I figure owls got the rest," he added.

I was ecstatic. Merganser ducks have a sharp beak with a serrated edge, totally unlike the flat, shovel-like bills of a mallard duck. They're fish-catchers, which we didn't realize at the time. Merganser ducks also have funny little haircuts: The feathers on top of their heads flip up at the back. To my eight-year-old eyes, they were beautiful.

But something was wrong. We kept trying to feed them grain, but they weren't taking it. The ducklings became sick and listless. My dad was frustrated. It looked as though he had saved the babies just to have them die in our care.

But finally, after Mom did some research on the little guys, she figured it out. "Fish," she said. "They eat fish."

We had a small stream, which we called a slough, that ran behind our house. Our nickname for it was "the Amazon." Our Amazon wasn't full of piranha, but minnows, small fingerlings that were gray and under an inch or two long. I'd help my dad catch a couple hundred every day, and the ducklings ate them with relish. I also went out with my dad at night to catch fat, juicy night crawlers to supplement their diet.

It was comical to watch the tiny little merganser ducks as they grabbed a half-foot-long night crawler to try to down it. Though the duckling was determined to swallow the night crawler, the worm was equally determined not to be swallowed. The night crawler wiggled ferociously, in a way that would force the duckling to completely contort its whole body. The duck wriggled and writhed, the worm writhed and struggled, and finally the duck would win and sit there happily with a full crop. It was the funniest sight.

That small flock of mergansers was so special to me because we didn't have any pets. They knew me, they would come up to me when I called, and they would nuzzle me with their tiny beaks. I wanted to keep them forever. But I had to learn an important lesson about wildlife. My dad used my room as an example.

"Look around," he said. In my bedroom was everything that I loved—my nice soft bed, my favorite toys, and great big sunny windows. I loved my room.

"I want you to imagine something," said

my dad. "Imagine if you could never leave this room. We'd bring in all your favorite food, and maybe you could have a TV and radio in here, but you still couldn't ever leave. Would you be happy?"

I knew what he was getting at. "Maybe for a little while," I replied.

"For a little while," he repeated.

We introduced the ducks back into the wild. Afterward, I thought about how it all made sense to me. No matter how nice the place is where you live, you need to experience life and the world.

It wouldn't be long before I'd learn another lesson that was a real turning point. I saw a dog scrounging around in the school parking lot, a dirty and scrawny mutt that had evidently been on his own for a while. Some of the kids and I shared a bit of food with the dog at recess. By the time classes were starting again we had befriended the poor thing.

I suddenly felt an unusual responsibility toward the stray. I didn't feel it was enough just to give it something to eat and say that I'd helped it, and then move on. I needed to make sure that dog was in a safe place.

"We've got to do something to help," I said to my teacher.

"The school's already called animal control," my teacher explained. She assured me that if the owners were looking for the stray, they would have the best chance of finding it through animal control.

I was stubborn. "But after a period of time, if the dog isn't claimed, they'll put it to sleep, right?"

My teacher nodded reluctantly. "I suppose."

"So that's not good enough."

My teacher sighed, giving me an I-haven't-got-time-for-this look. "There aren't really any other options, Terri."

And that was that. What happened to the stray dog, I'll never know. But with the fierce determination of a child to right injustice, I resolved that when I grew up, I would no longer turn a blind eye and walk past a problem. I would stop and fix it. I remember that episode very clearly as a defining moment in my life.

Neither the stray dog nor the ducklings were huge events, just minor incidents in the life of a young girl growing up in the Pacific Northwest. But they formed two vital threads in the fabric of who I am today: *When you help an animal, do your absolute best to make sure you don't harm it at the same time,* and *Never walk past a problem with an animal—fix it.*

These were the lessons I remembered when I encountered a sick, emaciated cougar in a plastic pet cage.

I started by contacting the Oregon Department of Fish and Wildlife. "Is it legal to keep a cougar?" I asked. It turned out that it was perfectly legal, provided the animal was born in captivity.

"Once they are in captivity," said the voice on the other end of the line, "they no longer fall under the jurisdiction of the Fish and Wildlife Department. They become the jurisdiction of the United States Department of Agriculture."

The bureaucrat's favorite strategy: Pass a problem on down the line.

I called the USDA and eventually found that there was only a single official, Dr. Overton, who was in charge of all of northern California and the entire 97,000 square miles of Oregon. His jurisdiction included every wild animal in captivity, from circus animals and roadside zoos to aquariums and even backyard pets.

I described the baby cougar's situation to him.

"The best we could do for the animal," he told me, "is to issue a warning and check up on her in a few months."

"In a few days, much less a few months, that cougar will be dead," I said.

"I apologize," Dr. Overton said. "I don't have any other options."

I felt bad for him, and I shared his frustration at being stretched so thin. The problem was bigger than both of us, and I hadn't even been aware of it. It reminded me of what my teacher had said about the stray dog. Back then, I swore that if there were no other options, then *I* would be the option. Now I was an adult with the opportunity to fix the glitch in this system.

I drove back up to Hillsboro, laid my money down, and took possession of one very sick, very pitiful cougar, pet pack and all.

As I pulled out of the parking lot, the man in the aviator glasses walked alongside my car, shouting advice. "You can tie her in the backyard like a dog. And they're really good with children. They're not destructive in a house. You can just bring them in and out, like you would treat a pet."

Right. A new pet. I thought about that as I drove the hundred miles south from Portland to Eugene, the baby cougar crying pitifully in her cage in the backseat.

My very first hurdle was that I already had a pet, a dog named Shasta who I dearly loved. I'd gotten her three years before, during a "Beachcombing Days" celebration near my parents' cabin on the Oregon coast. There was a little girl and her hippie mother, and they had a wagonload of puppies.

"They're free or they're two dollars," the young girl said as I walked past her.

I laughed out loud, and I don't know what came over me, but I gave her two dollars for a reddish brown puppy, a Border collie–golden retriever–Rhodesian ridgeback mix. I was drinking a soda pop called Shasta at the time, and I loved Mount Shasta, the majestic peak near the Oregon-California border.

Shasta the dog was most perturbed when I showed up at "her" house with a baby cougar. But she settled down after a few days, and the two had a sort of uneasy truce.

I still had to deal with the overwhelming feeling of "Now what am I going to do?" The baby cougar stayed in the garage. I played with her in the backyard and rolled around with her in the house. After a few days of eating good food, she started coming around and immediately began acting like a cougar. This turned out to be both good and bad.

Her greatest joy and favorite game was hiding until my back was turned. Then she'd pounce ferociously and grapple me around the backs of my legs. Cougars are superb stalk-and-ambush predators. Her cub-level version of it was a cute enough trick, unless I happened to be sitting down, not paying attention.

When I was doing paperwork, watching TV, or reclining in any sort of seated position, she would sneak up on me very quietly with her big, soft, padded feet on the carpet. I would never hear her coming. She would leap through the air and land on my back, grabbing the back of my neck with her jaws, pretending I was a wild white-tailed deer.

She would clamp down on me, refusing to let go, with a guttural growl coming out between her clenched teeth. The whole process left me rather unsettled. I never knew when I was going to be pounced on. I reflected on Aviator-Man's idea of having a cougar as a house pet and wondered how many people he had endangered. Sometimes, no matter how much you love someone, being roommates just isn't going to pan out.

I began doing more thorough and appropriate research. I learned that in spite of the fact that scores of wild animals were in the pet trade, no official regulations existed for housing a cougar. Several governmental agencies had opinions. The Department of Fish and Wildlife decided they had jurisdiction because a cougar was a native Oregonian animal. The USDA felt it had jurisdiction because I had the animal in captivity. The local county animal authorities also wanted to get involved. Everyone seemed to have their best guess as to what might be required. In the end, I figured it would be best to go along with the strictest guidelines.

I needed to build a four-hundred-square-foot enclosure, with a curbed concrete-slab floor six inches thick. The fence needed to be five-gauge cyclone fencing. I contacted several building companies and discovered that no manufacturer had made five-gauge cyclone fencing since World War II.

I wound up building a mini Fort Knox—which cost about six thousand dollars—in my backyard. I began furnishing it. The den box was huge, made of wood, bolted down off the ground, with a big rubber top. I put in a large picnic table. The cougar enjoyed that, since it was wood and she could leap up in two little steps to get on top. Then I hired another builder to put a roof over half the enclosure.

The money disappeared quickly. I learned that it cost about five dollars a day to feed this "ideal pet," and that the bigger she got, the more she enjoyed the pouncing game.

Fortunately, I didn't have to come up with a name for her, since she already came with a beautiful one—Malina. Instead of letting her jump on my head whenever she felt like it, I sought guidance on how to discipline her. I would let her play with me until she gave me a nip or grabbed me with her big feet and pulled me in for a good bite. Then I would scold her and pop her gently on the nose. We got to know each other, and Malina began to respect me. She soon became very territorial about her enclosure, and that's where Shasta came in.

Shasta was a brilliant sidekick. She would go into Malina's enclosure and find any little scraps of meat that might be left over after dinner. Malina didn't appreciate this much, but every time she tried to defend her territory, Shasta would bark, growl, and snap, quickly putting the cougar in her place. Soon Malina realized she wasn't top dog, and her attitude problems were quickly resolved.

She would sit passively in the corner and look slightly annoyed as Shasta went through every square inch looking for little scraps. This turned out to keep Malina in check and made the situation a lot safer as I came and went, cleaning her enclosure.

Malina also learned that it was fun to go out for walks on her leash. I took her everywhere. Early in the morning we would hit the local playground. The fences of the tennis courts were high enough that I could let her run around freely. Utilizing a thirty-foot lead, I'd also take her to the beach. Although Oregon beaches are usually quite deserted, occasionally a beachcomber would pass by us. Malina crawled on her belly as close to the stranger as she dared. She hid in the beach grass, flattening her ears to the side, looking like a funny cougar airplane, and would sit absolutely motionless.

People strolled by, and we would exchange hellos, but they never knew that three feet away from them was a crouching cougar.

Soon I was taking Malina out for events to educate people about cougars. She came with me to schools—everything from small classrooms to universities—and I would take her to various community events too. She loved it! She'd sit behind a roped-off area, flicking her tail, people-watching. I found it dismaying when a classroom full of children would see her and cry out, "Look at the tiger!" or "Look at the cheetah!" No one seemed to know what a cougar was, and yet Malina's wild cousins literally lived in our own Oregon backyards.

I began taking my cougar with me to court hearings. I'd join environmentalist attorneys and concerned people about the cruelty of certain hunting practices, such as bear baiting and hunting cougars with dogs.

By taking Malina into the courtroom, I not only got press, I brought the hunters face-to-face with the animal they were trying to persecute. Instead of the snarling, terrifying demon of the night that they imagined stalking their children, they would see a beautiful, noble spirit of the wilderness. Malina changed people's minds. I saw it happen.

Malina marked the beginning of my affinity for predatory mammals. After an internship with the Department of Fish and Wildlife, I earned my certificate as a wildlife rehabilitator. I had found my purpose. I didn't realize that within the next few months I would almost pay for it with my life.

CHAPTER THREE

Rescue

Soon more enclosures began to sprout up in my backyard. As a wildlife rehabilitator, I took in foxes, bobcats, raccoons, and possums. All sorts of animals came into my care, but I seemed to have a knack with predatory mammals above all others—with the exception of wolves. For some reason I never connected with wolves, but that didn't stop me from trying to help them.

One timber wolf I was called to rescue was beautiful but extraordinarily thin. She'd just had a litter of pups and was nursing them inside a mobile home. Somehow she got out of the trailer and was separated from her babies. The owners weren't home, and she could hear her pups crying inside. She systematically (and frantically) went around to every entrance to the trailer. Using her immense jaw pressure, she flattened all the doorknobs, tore off the window screens, and shredded the sides of the trailer trying to get back to her puppies.

"She destroyed our home," the wolf's owner told me over the phone. "She's got to go."

I put the wolf and her pups inside a dog kennel in my backyard. She immediately decided she didn't want to be in there. She grabbed the side of the cage in her jaws. Even though the kennel was seven feet wide and fourteen feet long, and had a roof on it, she started tugging until she pulled the cage partially off the concrete pad. At sixty pounds, probably half her normal weight, and lactating, the wolf was still demolishing her enclosure. I wasn't going to be able to hold her.

By now it was dark, and I didn't have many options. I knew I couldn't put her in the garage, since she would destroy it just as she had her former trailer home.

I thought of the one place she couldn't escape—my very own Fort Knox.

Wolf and cougar switched places. I moved Malina into the dog kennel and put the wolf and her pups in the four-hundred-square-foot cougar enclosure. I enticed the mama wolf away with some food so I could check on her puppies. The tiny wolf pups, whose eyes weren't even open yet, growled menacingly at my approach. They hated me without even seeing me.

Malina wasn't too thrilled with the new developments either. She didn't like her new small enclosure, but I was too busy to notice. After all, it was only going to be a few days until I placed the wolf and her puppies with a rescue group that specialized in wolves. That weekend, I drove up the coast and left them in much better hands than mine.

It had been a big day. I returned home after dark and went in to feed and brush Malina—our usual evening routine. She sat up on her den box inside the small enclosure. As I was brushing her, she put her forehead down to me as she always did, asking for a bit of a rub. As part of this process, Malina would usually bump her head into mine. It always hurt a bit, but it was a sign of affection, so I bumped heads back.

When I turned around to walk out of the enclosure, without warning, Malina pounced.

All of a sudden, I felt her muscular forearms enveloping my shoulders. It was like being in the grip of a full-grown man. She grabbed the back of my head so that her upper teeth dug into the top of my skull, with her bottom canines hooked neatly under the lip of my skull at the back of my neck.

Malina began to bite down, and the pressure was intense. I could feel her canines puncturing my scalp. My head was going to explode. Her arms braced my shoulders, squeezing tightly. I had nothing to fight her off with. I started swinging wildly backward with the brush in my hand, hitting her on the top of the head. She didn't budge. The pressure grew so great that I knew something was going to give.

"NO, NO, NO!" I yelled at the top of my lungs. She loosened her grip for a moment and I quickly twisted away. She dropped down to the floor of the kennel but immediately pounced again, grappling me around the front and biting at my chest. I beat her away a second time and backed for the door.

Malina assumed her pounce position once more, with her tail wiggling and her rump swaying back and forth.

I felt the adrenaline surging through my arms and into my fingertips as I reached behind me and fumbled with the latch. It was tricky, but I didn't dare turn around. I managed to unlatch the door and slam it behind me. I collapsed. I had not an ounce of strength left. I felt sick.

With a huge, booming bang, Malina crashed into the door just after it shut. She turned around, gave me a dirty look over her shoulder, and sulked back to her den box.

I learned a few valuable lessons that night. First of all, I needed to be really careful about working with wild animals when I was by myself. Second, never take an animal that is used to one enclosure and put it in a smaller one. And last, a wild animal is just that. You can never tame them or train them. I could work with them and develop some level of mutual respect. But I could never forget they were wild.

I was more or less prepared for the physical aspects of wildlife rescue. I never shied away from hard work. My father always worked multiple jobs when I was growing up—I respected him for it and modeled my work ethic on his. As I took on more and more rescue work, I was also still running my pilot car company, Westates Flagman.

So physical challenges I could face. But I found myself less prepared for the emotional challenges of the rescue work I was taking on. The way some people treat wildlife is beyond comprehension.

A cougar hunted by dogs is put through unbelievable trauma. I didn't think I could possibly understand what the terror must be like, but I got some idea from a friend who worked with predatory mammals and who was also a Vietnam vet.

"In the war," he told me, "the Vietcong used to hunt the American soldiers with dogs." It was terrifying, he said. He knew he was being hunted, and he knew he couldn't escape. He spent a lot of time running through streams, backtracking, trying to escape the relentless dogs. These were animals that tracked not only by sight; they could also smell, hear, and sense your presence.

Instead of just hating the hunters, I tried to learn from them. I went to hunting exhibitions and fairground events. I learned that a mother cougar will climb a tree when a hunter approaches, leaving her cubs to be torn apart by hunting dogs. A cougar's fear of humans is so great it outweighs her instinct to protect her young. The stories were heartbreaking, but in some ways these people knew more about cougars than I did.

Still, the more I learned, the more determined I became to stop these wildlife perpetrators. I would even sit in on court cases to show support and encouraged others to do the same, especially with truly heinous crimes against wildlife. For one memorable trial, the judge moved the venue three times to increasingly larger courtrooms, because there were three hundred of us who showed up.

On trial were two men, one in a plaid shirt, and the other with a long, ZZ Top–style beard. They looked intimidated by the crowd that had turned out, even though Plaid Shirt stood six foot four. He was the main perpetrator, charged with animal cruelty. He had brought his young son along during the bear killing for which he was on trial.

The main reason the state managed to bring charges is that the hunters had made a videotape of their gruesome acts. The state trooper who confiscated the video couldn't even testify at the time of the trial, he was so emotionally overcome.

Then they showed the video in court, and I understood why. ZZ Top and Plaid Shirt cornered the bear cub. In order to preserve the integrity of the pelt, they attempted to kill the cub by stabbing it in the eyes.

It was absolutely gut-wrenching to watch. The bear struggled for its life, but Plaid Shirt kept thrusting his knife, moving back as the animal twisted frantically away, then moving forward to stab again. The bear cub screamed, and it sounded eerily as though the bear was actually crying "Mama," over and over. Plaid Shirt and ZZ Top sat unfazed in court. The bear screamed, "Mama, mama, mama." From my place in the gallery, I watched as a towering man in a police uniform burst into tears and walked out of the courtroom. At the end of the video, Plaid Shirt brought his nine-year-old son over to stand triumphantly next to the dead bear cub.

"Clearly, you deserve jail," the judge told Plaid Shirt as he stood for sentencing. "Unfortunately, the jails are filled with people even more heinous than you: rapists, murderers, and armed robbers. So I am going to sentence you to three thousand hours of community service."

I approached the judge after the trial, furious that this man might end up collecting a bit of rubbish along the highway as his penance.

"I want him," I said, referring to Plaid Shirt. I said that I ran a wildlife rehabilitation facility and could use a volunteer.

The first day Plaid Shirt showed up, he actually looked scared of me. He cleaned cages, fed animals, and worked hard. He liked the bobcat I was taking care of, "Bobby." He said it was the biggest one he had ever seen. It would make a prize trophy.

I asked him every question I could think of: where he hunted, how he hunted, why he hunted. Whether he had any kind of shirt other than plaid. I felt as though I was in the presence of true evil.

For months he helped. He had some skills, like carpentry, and he could lift heavy things. He fulfilled his community service. In the end, I couldn't tell if I had made any difference or not. I was only slightly encouraged by his parting words.

"You know," Plaid Shirt said, "I never knew cougars purred."

* * * *

The emotional roller coaster of rescue work never seemed to end. I named my facility "Cougar Country" to highlight my focus, but I found myself called to help many different animals—in veterinarians' offices, in the field, in classrooms and courtrooms. Somehow I kept it all together, and ran Westates Flagman, too. My day had forty-eight hours.

It helped that I had no social life. I recall a poor fellow who asked me out during this period. I agreed to meet him for dinner. As I was getting ready, the phone rang.

"We've got a possum that's been hit by a car," the county animal control office said. "Can you help?"

I've always liked possums. Like a lot of wildlife, they are completely misunderstood. Virginia opossums are the only North American marsupials. Marsupials tend to have lower body temperatures than other animals, so possums are among the least likely of any mammal to contract rabies. In fact, they are one of the most disease-free animals I've dealt with.

That evening, answering the call as I dressed for my big date, I didn't think twice. I thought I could pick it up and still make dinner. But when I got the injured possum home and examined it, I realized that it had probably been hit by the car two or three days earlier, and its body teemed with maggots.

There wasn't any way I could head out for a lovely evening, not with a maggot-infested marsupial under my care. I grabbed my tweezers and began flicking off the fly larvae, one by one. The possum was cooperative, but as the maggot-picking process wore on, it became evident that I was not going to able to make dinner.

I called the fellow. "Here's the situation," I said. "I am working on a possum that was hit by a car. There is just no way I am going to be on time. What do you want to do?"

There was a long hesitation on the other end of the line.

"Why don't I come over and help?" he finally asked. Great! I could always use help. A half hour later, in he came, looking smart and smelling of cologne.

His face immediately turned pale as he saw what the project entailed, and he made a halfhearted attempt to help. After a while I wasn't sure whether I was going to be finishing up with the possum or providing medical aid for my poor date, whose face had now turned a whiter shade of green. He excused himself and headed off into the night, never to be heard from again.

Life was rewarding but hectic. After a particularly long day, I got a phone call out of the blue.

"I'm going to Australia to scuba dive the Great Barrier Reef," my friend Lori said to me in September of 1991. "You ought to come along. We'd have a great time."

My first thought was to pass. Diving had never interested me. I couldn't shake the feeling that it just wasn't natural to breathe underwater.

"I know you'll have a good time," I told Lori, "but scuba's not really my thing."

Lori was persistent. "Yeah, I know I'll have a good time," she said, "but you'd have a good time too. You *need* a good time."

A lot of things argued against this trip. I thought of tortured bears, sick raccoons, and the endless parade of injured and abused animals that passed through my care. My backyard was full of rescued animals that needed care and attention, 24/7. And I knew the key to running my business was being there every single day. I loved my life, but maybe Lori had a point. I had been burning the candle at both ends and some in the middle.

"I've got a girlfriend over there," Lori continued, trying to convince me. "We'd have someone to hang out with who knows the country."

I'd been to Australia once in my early twenties, journeying up the coast from Sydney to Brisbane, seeing everything in between: a Mostly Mozart concert at the Sydney Opera House, a beautiful old cemetery, pet wombats and tame kangaroos, the surf and sea at Great Keppel Island. It was the most wonderful place I had ever visited. I had fallen in love with the wildlife, the wild places, and the open, friendly people.

And there were the cougars. In the back of my mind I thought I might be able to combine my passion for rescue work with my love of Australia. Cougars had always been my focus, the reason I had started on the path I was traveling.

Cougar Country was taking in cougars from everywhere: when they were raised as pets but discarded, when they grew too dangerous, and when they were orphaned by hunters. I couldn't keep them all myself. I needed responsible facilities to take them. Completely naive about Australia's importation and quarantine regulations, I nevertheless thought that surely there might be some opportunities down under for people doing educational work with wildlife, who might be able to take a cougar.

Visiting Australia again, I thought, might not be a bad idea. How could I have known then that my decision would result, only a short time later, in a chance meeting with the man who would change my life?

CHAPTER FOUR

Burdekin

After meeting Steve for the first time in the Queensland heat, I arrived back home to a cool, foggy Oregon in the fall of 1991. Malina and Cougar Country were waiting, and my old life quickly swept me up. But the world had changed. *I* had changed.

A week passed, then two. By the third week I was pretty sure I wasn't going to hear from my Australian action hero ever again. But there wasn't a day that went by when he wasn't the first thing on my mind as I woke up, and the last thing on my mind as I went to sleep. It was almost as though he wasn't real, and everything that had happened had been a dream.

After four weeks of waiting for a call from Australia, I became convinced that it wasn't going to happen. I wasn't going to call him; it would be pointless. I didn't have the time or the money to flit off to Australia again. If Steve wanted to talk to me, he would have found a way.

I really missed him.

In mid-November of that year, a call came in at ten o'clock at night. Late-night calls back then always made my heart skip a beat, because my first thought was that it might be Steve. It wasn't. A woman had discovered a kitten that had fallen down a storm drain and was now trapped beneath an impossibly heavy grate. Could I come?

I was tired, and it was late. It was another disappointing phone call—it wasn't Steve. "Take a long piece of cloth, something like a bedsheet," I told her wearily. "Tie knots in it every few inches and lower it down. See what happens. If it works, the kitten should start climbing up the bedsheet and come to you."

The woman promised to try it. I grabbed a quick shower and went to bed, falling into a deep, dream-filled sleep.

The phone rang, jolting me awake. Not Steve this time, either, but my friend the kitten woman.

"It worked," she gushed. "She's okay!"

I looked blearily at the clock—it was approaching midnight. I shut my eyes and let myself drift back to Australia, the warm sun, the tropical nights, and the huge fruit bats flying across star-studded skies.

Once again, the jangle of the phone jolted me upright. Not again! Now what did she want? Reluctantly I picked up the receiver.

"G'day, mate," said the voice on the other end of the line. "It's Stevo calling from Australia. How you going?"

Well, for starters, I was going without breathing for a few moments. "Good," I stammered. Luckily, I didn't have to talk, because Steve started right in on what was going on with the zoo.

"The weather is heating up and the crocs will be laying soon," he said, and I could barely hear him over the pounding of my heart.

"I've got a chance to take a little time before summer hits," he added.

I waited for what seemed like a long beat, still breathless.

"I'm coming to Oregon in ten days," he said. "I'd really love to see you."

Yes! I was floored. Ten days. That would be . . . Thanksgiving.

"Steve," I said, "do you know about the American holiday of Thanksgiving?"

"Too right," he said cheerfully, but it was obvious that he didn't.

"We all get together as a family," I explained. "We eat our brains out and take walks and watch a lot of football—American football, you know, gridiron, not your rugby league football."

I was babbling. "Do you want to come and share Thanksgiving with my family?"

Steve didn't seem to notice my fumbling tongue. "I'd be happy to," he answered. "That'd be brilliant."

"Great," I said.

"Great," he said.

"Send me all the details, your flight and everything," I said.

"I will," he promised. Then he hung up. As suddenly as he was there, he was gone.

I sat on the edge of my bed for a long time that night, trying to convince myself that it hadn't been a dream. Steve had called, and now he was coming to see me.

This was going to be fabulous.

* * * *

Thanksgiving Day finally arrived. I remember feeling so proud to have my family meet my Aussie man. We had just eaten an epic feast of deviled eggs, turkey and stuffing, lots of gravy, cranberry sauce, sweet potatoes, and soft rolls with stacks of butter. We took a break before the desserts came out, and the menfolk headed into the living room to watch football. But Steve wandered back into the kitchen where I was helping to clear the dishes and clean up. He took the time to talk to each of my sisters and my mom, getting to know the whole family.

I thought he was very considerate, because I knew instinctively that this wasn't so easy for him. He was a bit shy, and totally out of his element. He had never visited the United States before, or been this serious about a girl. We had spent only a few days with each other, but both of us seemed to know that his visit was more than just a casual meeting. Being together felt more and more like destiny.

We went everywhere. I gave him the grand tour, the best the Pacific Northwest has to offer, which is nothing short of spectacular. Everything revolved around wildlife. We hiked the Coast Range out of my parents' beach cabin to look for black bears, and traveled to eastern Oregon to see white-tailed deer, coyotes, and the eastern Oregon antelope, animals that Steve had never experienced before.

He skied Mount Bachelor. I wasn't much of a skier, so I went off to track down wildlife while he had a great time on the slopes. Meeting him at the lodge afterward, I had to head off a leggy blonde who was intent on teaching Steve how to use an American pay phone. Not the kind of wildlife I was interested in him experiencing.

We returned to Eugene, and I showed him where I worked part-time at an emergency veterinary hospital. He was particularly impressed with an injured porcupine that had come in, shedding some quills. Instead of just looking at them, Steve, with his usual enthusiasm, jabbed one into his arm.

"What are you doing?" I asked, even though it was obvious.

"I just wanted to see what it would feel like," he said.

"So how does it feel?"

"Really painful," he said. He sounded impressed. I couldn't help laughing. He felt the reverse barbs on the quill work themselves into his skin. It was quite a flesh-ripping experience to pull the quill back out.

Then, too soon, our time was over. I felt the familiar ache, the pressure in the middle of my chest. Ever since I'd met Steve, I had experienced the same ache whenever I left him. It was a very real pain, one I'd never felt before.

"I have to see you again," I said. For the first time, I was very open about my feelings for him. As he was leaving, I was already making plans to see him again in Australia.

I left the icebox cold of Oregon for the tropical heat of Cairns in early January 1992. As I got off the plane to catch my connecting flight to Brisbane, I found it almost difficult to breathe, it was so hot and muggy.

My mind was working in funny ways. *It's just too hot here,* I thought. *I could never live here.* Then I caught myself. *Hang on a minute. What was that? Why would that even be an option, living here? I'm just coming over to see this guy.* But that Cairns moment was the first time I actually thought about leaving my Oregon life behind to join Steve in his Australian one.

On my final approach to Brisbane, I had

an excited feeling again, a sense of coming home. It seemed like I was the only passenger eager to get off the plane. Everyone else was moving as though they were underwater. I stepped out into the airport. There was Steve, back in his khakis. It was nice to see him in those familiar shorts again, after having to bundle up in Oregon against the cold.

We embraced, and I had the sense that we were one person. Apart, we weren't whole, but together, we were okay again.

We immediately got lost in conversation. The crocodiles were nesting, Steve said. It was stinking hot, the perfect time of year for all things reptilian. Steve Irwin's time.

At first we stayed close to home. Steve put me up at the Irwin home on the zoo grounds, rather than the little motel up the road. We hit the ground running. Twenty-four hours after I stepped off the plane in Brisbane, Steve was showing me how to raid croc nests to retrieve the eggs so they wouldn't just die in the nest.

He showed me how to feed venomous snakes that were hot and loaded, how to get in with the cassowaries and retrieve their food bucket without getting kicked in half. Steve could gently lift a python out of its enclosure in order to clean it. I would reach in, in what I considered to be exactly the same way, and immediately get bitten three times before I knew what hit me.

I slowly got to know the staff, who were more like extended family, and Steve's remarkable parents. They had founded the zoo nearly a quarter century before. Steve's father, Bob, still did the books. His mom ran the food kiosk, and she delivered up delicious sandwiches and the most incredible raspberry slices on the planet. Steve's best mate, Wes Mannion, was working as his right-hand man.

As much as I enjoyed it, we weren't going to stay at the zoo for long. I was about to experience a life-changing event: Steve Irwin in the Australian bush.

Our destination was the Burdekin River, on the coast, eight hundred miles north of Brisbane. The Burdekin is a magic river, dependent on the wet season, which brings floods of epic proportions. The rainfall in the area is massively unpredictable and wholly cyclone-dependent. The Burdekin was the closest habitat to the zoo for the big saltwater crocs, so off to the river we went.

Dams were planned, Steve explained.

The river wasn't terribly well known, and its crocodile populations weren't well understood. He wanted to go up and survey the crocs, see where their nesting sites were, and gauge the success of their breeding.

My first hurdle came before we even left. Steve's little dog Sui was coming with us, and she realized that I would be taking her place next to Steve in the front of the truck.

"Move over, Sui," I said. She turned and glared at me, for all the world like a jealous woman. I couldn't help but laugh. She was such a cute thing, and she looked at Steve with such rapture, joy, and love, that I had to forgive her for hating me.

I hadn't been much help packing for the trip. I was accustomed to America, where I was always within striking distance of a grocery store, gas station, or equipment supply. The Australian bush wasn't like that. Parts of the Burdekin were dangerously remote, and these, of course, were the parts where we were headed.

Steve had to pack his own fuel, water, food, spare tires, boat, engine, and extra parts. He loaded up the Ute. Swags went in, but no tent. We would be sleeping under the stars. As we headed out, it came to light that this would be a sixteen-hour trip—and the driving would be shared.

"Remember one thing," Steve said as he climbed over the seat. "If you see a road train coming, you've got to get clear off the road."

"Okay," I agreed. "But I need you to explain what a road train is." I learned that long-distance truckers in the outback drive huge rigs—double-deckers that are three trailers long.

"Okay, great," I said. "Drive on the left, and watch out for road trains. Got it." Steve climbed into the back under the canvas canopy and stretched out on top of one of the swags. I wasn't worried about falling asleep while I was driving. I was too nervous to be sleepy.

The farther north I drove, the smaller the roads became. Cars were few and far between. I saw the headlights of an oncoming Ute. *Maybe I'll practice pulling off the road,* I thought. I miscalculated the speed of the oncoming vehicle, slowed down more abruptly than I intended, and pulled completely onto the soft gravel shoulder.

The draft of the passing truck hit our Ute like a sonic boom—it was a giant beast with a huge welded bull bar on its front and triple trailers behind. The road train flew past us doing every bit of seventy-five miles per hour, never slowing down. I realized that if I hadn't pulled over, I would have probably been knocked off the face of the earth. I imagined a small paragraph buried deep inside the *Eugene Register-Guard,* my hometown newspaper: "Oregon Woman Bites the Dust." Road trains owned the road, but I had passed my first test. I could do this!

I should not have spoken so soon.

Steve drove the next morning as we made the turn for the Burdekin River. The single-lane dirt road, as small as it was, ended there—but we had another two or three hours of four-wheel driving to go. We navigated through deep ravines carved by the area's repeated cyclone-fed floods, occasionally balancing on three wheels.

"Hang out the window, will you?" Steve shouted as we maneuvered around the edge of a forty-foot drop. "I need to you to help counterbalance the truck."

You've got to be kidding me, I thought. But there I was, hanging off the side of the bull bar while Steve threaded his way over the eroding track.

As we pounded and slammed our way deep into the bush, Steve talked about the area's Aborigines. He pointed out a butte where European colonists massacred a host of the Aboriginal population in Victorian times. The landscape was alive to him, not only with human history, but with the complex interrelatedness of plants, animals, and the environment. He pointed out giant 150-year-old eucalypts, habitats for insectivorous bats, parrots, and brush-tailed possums.

After hours of bone-jarring terrain, we reached the Burdekin, a beautiful river making its way through the tea trees. It was a breathtaking place. We set up camp—by which I mean Steve did—at a fork in the river, where huge black boulders stood exposed in the middle of the water.

I tried to help, but I felt completely out of my depth. He unpacked the boat and the motor, got it tied and moored on the river, rolled out the swags, and lined up containers of fuel, water, and food.

Then he started stringing tarps. What a gift Steve had for setting up camp. He had done it countless times before, month in and month out, all by himself, with only Sui for company. I watched him secure ropes, tie knots, and stretch canvas like he was expecting that we'd have to withstand a cyclone. It was hot, more than a hundred degrees Fahrenheit, but Steve didn't seem to notice.

Sui found a little shallow place at the edge of the river and immediately plopped herself in. I saw Steve look over at her as if calculating her chances of being snatched by a croc. Crocodiles are the ultimate camouflage attack predators, striking from the water's edge.

There would never be "down time" for Steve. No time to sit down and unwind. We were off in an instant. We grabbed Sui, jumped in the boat, and headed upstream. White Burdekin ducks startled up in front of our boat, their dark neck-rings revealed as they flew over us. Cormorants dried their feathers on the mid-river boulders, wings fully open. It was magical and unspoiled, as if we were the first people ever to travel there.

Steve knew the area intimately. As part of the East Coast Crocodile Management Program in the 1980s, he had been commissioned to remove problem crocodiles. People often wanted to frequent crocodile water, and the crocs were inevitably the losers.

Crocodiles helped maintain the ecological balance, which meant that wherever there were crocodiles, there was great fishing. Therein lay the conflict. Fishermen didn't seem to like sharing their favorite spot with a crocodile. All through the decade, Steve caught and relocated numerous Burdekin River crocs. He even had some at the Queensland Reptile and Fauna Park that he'd gotten from this very river.

Burdekin crocodiles were special, and physically different from other salties, a bit more sleek and streamlined. Many of them had only four nuchal scutes, the osteodermal plates on the neck, while most saltwater crocs had six. As we motored up the river, Steve pointed out slides and footprints left behind by crocodiles that had been sunning on the bank. The farther upstream we went, the bigger the slides got.

Steve explained the social hierarchy of the crocodile. Each group has their own territory: Females would inhabit a specific area to nest, and then there would be big male salties. The subadult crocs dwelled on the fringe, staying out of the way of the big dominant crocs. There were also "crèche areas," where the baby crocs would grow up, catching small insects, fish, frogs, or baby birds.

We returned to camp. Steve seemed calmer now that he'd gone up the river, gotten his bearings, and revisited familiar places. Just downstream from the camp, we hopped from one exposed boulder to the next, getting out into the middle of the river. I didn't know what to expect. I still wasn't completely sure of what crocodiles could do. I was pretty confident that they couldn't fly, but beyond that, I didn't know. I relied on Steve.

As we sat together on a mid-river boulder, the shadows crossed the water and the sun sank lower. We looked into each other's eyes and talked about all the things we loved. I realized then that there was no turning back: I had fallen in love with Steve. As the sun set, we made our way back across the boulders before it got dark.

"Nighttime is croc time," Steve told me. "It's important to get off the water before they are active and hunting."

Back in camp, Steve started cooking. I asked if I could help. He waved me off. "My trip, my treat," he said.

I sat with my lemonade and watched the river as it changed with darkness coming on, and enjoyed the smell of onions cooking and steaks frying. I could hear the soft flapping noise of the fruit bats overhead. At first there were just a few, then dozens, and finally hundreds, crossing above the crowns of paperbark trees and honey myrtles. In the last glimmer of light they looked surreal, spooky and beautiful, gliding across the darkening sky.

I felt pleasantly tired, but Steve seemed more energized the longer we stayed in the bush. I would see it again and again over the years. This was where Steve belonged, and where he seemed most alive.

We finished dinner, and Steve popped the dishes into the dishpan. "Right," he said. "We'll leave them to soak and come back to clean up later."

We jumped into the boat and headed back up the river. This was Steve's favorite time. I hadn't understood what he was doing on our first trip earlier that afternoon. He had memorized where he had seen the slides. While during the day we hadn't spotted a single croc, almost immediately after getting on the water, Steve shone his spotlight across the inky blackness and picked up the red eye-shine of crocs.

As we slowly idled the boat upstream, the red orbs would blink and then vanish as the crocodiles submerged on our approach. Suddenly I felt terribly exposed in the little dinghy. The beautiful melaleuca trees that had looked so spectacular during the day now hung eerily over the water, as their leaves dipped and splashed in the black water. Fish came alive too. Everything made more noise in the dark.

As Steve glided along the edge of the overhanging leaves, every now and then a golden orb spiderweb would clutch at my hair, the thick, yellow, sticky webbing covering my head, the boat, and the torch. Steve was oblivious to anything but the crocodiles.

Some of them allowed us to get close. Steve could gauge a croc's total size based on the length of its head. My heart kept pounding, and I tried to do everything right. He showed me how to hold the spotlight right under my chin, so that I could look directly over the beam and pick up the eyeshine of the crocs. I was tired, yet adrenaline surged through my veins.

"Look, look, look," Steve whispered excitedly, "there's another one." There was something strange about this one, only a single red eye reflected. Perhaps the other one had been shot out, Steve suggested.

"He's big," he whispered. "Maybe fifteen feet."

We edged closer. The engine coughed and suddenly ground to a stop. Steve leaned over the back of the dinghy, reaching in up to his shoulder in the water, to clear the weeds from around the propeller.

The single red eye blinked out. The big croc had submerged. *Submerged where?* I thought. Steve finally cleared the weeds and yanked the ignition cord, but the engine refused to turn over.

I am in the middle of nowhere. It's nighttime. I am surrounded by crocodiles. The boat motor won't start. Steve will be snatched and eaten by One-Eye right off the back of the boat. Then I'll be alone.

But after some gentle persuasion (some of it verbal, and not so gentle), the engine finally started. The heat hadn't really broken when we got back to camp. It was still well over ninety degrees. The insects that had been attracted to my spotlight were stuck and struggling in the sweat running down my back.

"How about a quick tub?" Steve said. That was Australian for bath. Somehow, the words "bath" and "crocodile" refused to go together in my mind.

But into the Burdekin we went, in our shorts, barefoot, picking our way through the stones, sticks, and burrs until we got to the smooth rocks of the river. Steve jumped in. I was more cautious. As I edged toward deeper water, he blocked my path and moved himself around in front of me.

"What are you doing?"

He laughed. "I caught the last big male crocodile around here last year, but I can't be too sure another one hasn't moved in."

"So," I said, "you want to make sure to keep yourself between me and the rest of the river."

"Right-o, mate," he replied.

I thought, *Is this guy for real?* Most guys think they're doing a girl a favor by opening a door, and here Steve was, putting himself between me and a croc.

* * * *

I avoided getting eaten on the Burdekin. I managed again to escape being flattened by a road train on the return trip to the zoo. My monthlong stay in Australia was nearing its end. The ache hadn't hit me yet, but I could feel it coming.

On our return from the bush, we went straight back to work at the zoo. A huge tree behind the Irwin family home had been hit by lightning some years previously, and a tangle of dead limbs was in danger of crashing down on the house. Steve thought it would be best to take the dead tree down.

I tried to lend a hand. Steve's mother could not watch as he scrambled up the tree. He had no harness, just his hat and a chainsaw. The tree was sixty feet tall. Steve looked like a little dot way up in the air, swinging through the tree limbs with an orangutan's ease, working the chainsaw.

Then it was my turn. After he pruned off all the limbs, the last task was to fell the massive trunk. Steve climbed down, secured a rope two-thirds of the way up the tree, and tied the other end to the bull bar of his Ute.

My job was to drive the Ute. "You're going to have to pull it down in just the right direction," he said, chopping the air with his palm. He studied the angle of the tree and where it might fall.

Steve cut the base of the tree. As the chainsaw snarled, Steve yelled, "Now!" I put the truck in reverse, slipped the clutch, and went backward at a forty-five-degree angle as hard as I could. With a groan and a tremendous crash, the tree hit the ground.

We celebrated, whooping and hollering. Steve cut the downed timber into lengths and I stacked it. The whole project took us all day. By late in the afternoon, my back ached from stacking tree limbs and logs. As the long shadows crossed the yard, Steve said four words very uncharacteristic of him: "Let's take a break."

I wondered what was up. We sat under a big fig tree in the yard with a cool drink. We were both covered in little flecks of wood, leaves, and bark. Steve's hair was unkempt, a couple of his shirt buttons were missing, and his shorts were torn. I thought he was the best-looking man I had ever seen in my life.

"I am not even going to walk for the next three days," I said, laughing.

Steve turned to me. He was quiet for a moment. "So, do you want to get married?"

Casual, matter-of-fact. I nearly dropped the glass I was holding. I had twigs in my hair and dirt caked on the side of my face. I'd taken off my hat, and I could feel my hair sticking to the sides of my head.

My first thought was what a mess I must look. My second, third, and fourth thoughts were lists of every excuse in the world why I couldn't marry Steve Irwin.

I could not possibly leave my job, my house, my wildlife work, my family, my friends, my pets—everything I had worked so hard for back in Oregon.

He never looked concerned. He simply held my gaze.

As all these things flashed through my mind, a little voice from somewhere above me spoke.

"Yes, I'd love to."

With those four words my life changed forever.

CHAPTER FIVE

The Crocodile Hunter

"What'll it be?" Steve asked me, just days after our wedding. "Do we go on the honeymoon we've got planned, or do you want to go catch crocs?"

My head was still spinning from the ceremony, the celebration, and the fact that I could now use the two words "my husband" and have them mean something real. The four months between February 2, 1992—the day Steve asked me to marry him—and our wedding day on June 4 had been a blur.

Steve's mother threw us an engagement party for Queensland friends and family, and I encountered a very common theme: "We never thought Steve would get married."

Everyone said it—relatives, old friends, and schoolmates. I'd smile and nod, but my inner response was, *Well, we've got that in common.* And something else: *Wait until I get home and tell everybody I am moving to Australia.*

I knew what I'd have to explain. Being with Steve, running the zoo, and helping the crocs was exactly the right thing to do. I knew with all my heart and soul that this was the path I was meant to travel. My American friends—the best, closest ones—understood this perfectly. I trusted Steve with my life and loved him desperately.

One of the first challenges was how to bring as many Australian friends and family as possible over to the United States for the wedding. None of us had a lot of money. Eleven people wound up making the trip from Australia, and we held the ceremony in the big Methodist church my grandmother attended.

It was more than a wedding, it was saying good-bye to everyone I'd ever known. I invited everybody, even people who may not have been intimate friends. I even invited my dentist. The whole network of wildlife rehabilitators came too—four hundred people in all.

The ceremony began at eight p.m., with coffee and cake afterward. I wore the same dress that my older sister Bonnie had worn at her wedding twenty-seven years earlier, and my sister Tricia wore at her wedding six years after that. The wedding cake had white frosting, but it was decorated with real flowers instead of icing ones.

Steve had picked out a simple ring for me, a quarter carat, exactly what I wanted. He didn't have a wedding ring. We were just going to borrow one for the service, but we couldn't find anybody with fingers that were big enough. It turned out that my dad's wedding ring fitted him, and that's the one we used. Steve's mother, Lyn, gave me a silk horseshoe to put around my wrist, a symbol of good luck.

On our wedding day, June 4, 1992, it had been eight months since Steve and I first met. As the minister started reading the vows, I could see that Steve was nervous. His tuxedo looked like it was strangling him. For a man who was used to working in the tropics, he sure looked hot. The church was air-conditioned, but sweat drops formed on the ends of his fingers. *Poor Steve,* I thought. He'd never been up in front of such a big crowd before.

"The scariest situation I've ever been in," Steve would say later of the ceremony. This from a man who wrangled crocodiles!

When the minister invited the groom to kiss the bride, I could feel all Steve's energy, passion, and love. I realized without a doubt we were doing the right thing.

Then, just as we were to leave on a whirlwind honeymoon in the beautiful Pacific Northwest, a call came from Australia. Steve's friend John Stainton had word that a big croc had been frequenting areas too close to civilization, and someone had been taking potshots at him.

"It's a big one, Stevo, maybe fourteen or fifteen feet," John said over the phone. "I hate to catch you right at this moment, but they're going to kill him unless he gets relocated."

John was one of Australia's award-winning documentary filmmakers. He and Steve had met in the late 1980s, when Steve would help John shoot commercials that required a zoo animal like a lizard or a turtle. But their friendship did not really take off until 1990, when an Australian beer company hired John to film a tricky shot involving a crocodile.

He called Steve. "They want a bloke to toss a coldie to another bloke, but a croc comes out of the water and snatches at it. The guy grabs the beer right in front of the croc's jaws. You think that's doable?"

"Sure, mate, no problem at all," Steve said with his usual confidence. "Only one thing, it has to be my hand in front of the croc."

John agreed. He journeyed up to the zoo to film the commercial. It was the first time he had seen Steve on his own turf, and he was impressed. He was even more impressed when the croc shoot went off flawlessly.

Monty, the saltwater crocodile, lay partially submerged in his pool. An actor fetched a coldie from the esky and tossed it toward Steve. As Steve's hand went above Monty's head, the crocodile lunged upward in a food response. On film it looked like the croc was about to snatch the can—which Steve caught right in front of his jaws. John was extremely impressed. As he left the zoo after completing the commercial shoot, Steve gave him a collection of VHS tapes.

Steve had shot the videotapes himself. The raw footage came from Steve simply propping his camera in a tree, or jamming it into the mud, and filming himself single-handedly catching crocs.

John watched the tapes when he got home to Brisbane. He told me later that what he saw was unbelievable. "It was three hours of captivating film and I watched it straight through, twice," John recalled to me. "It was Steve. The camera loved him."

He rang up his contacts in television and explained that he had a hot property. The programmers couldn't use Steve's original VHS footage, but one of them had a better idea. He gave John the green light to shoot his own documentary of Steve.

That led to John Stainton's call to Oregon on the eve of our honeymoon.

"I know it's not the best timing, mate," John said, "but we could take a crew and film a documentary of you rescuing this crocodile."

Steve turned to me. Honeymoon or crocodile? For him, it wasn't much of a quandary. But what about me?

"Let's go," I replied.

Two weeks after we said, "I do," Steve and I were on a river system called Cattle Creek, near Ingham, seven hundred miles up the Australian coast from Brisbane. John Stainton was along with a sound man and a cameraman. Steve's best mate, Wes, was there too.

The big saltie in Cattle Creek was in great danger. When we arrived, we immediately discovered cartridge casings and other evidence that people had been shooting at him from the shores of the river. Steve worked up and down the river system in the dinghy, finding the areas the crocodile had been frequenting, mentally marking the slides, and searching for the right spot to set the trap.

It seemed like only a few days ago I was in Oregon. What was I doing? I was out rescuing crocodiles with my new husband, and a film crew was documenting our every move. Newlywed, croc hunter, filmmaker: three brand-new job descriptions, hitting me all at once.

And cook. At the end of an exhausting

first day, the six of us—Steve, myself, Wes, John, and his two-person crew—gathered wearily around the fire. I looked up and realized that five pairs of eyes were looking at me. Wait a minute. Oh, I get it: I'm the only woman here. I am supposed to be cooking dinner.

The camp "kitchen" consisted of a collection of odd, alien-looking utensils such as a jaffle iron and a camp oven. I had no idea how to use any of them. Steve came to the rescue. He made toasted sandwiches in the jaffle iron and cooked up a stew in the camp oven. We realized it was going to work best if I was the assistant and he was the chef.

Mosquitoes came off the river in clouds. Every once in a while goannas sauntered right through camp. As I chopped vegetables that first night, a big lacey showed up.

"Grab it," Steve said to me. I dropped what I was doing and picked up the lizard. John and his crew went into action. I told the camera everything I knew about lace monitors.

"Lace monitors are excellent tree climbers," I said. "They can grow up to seven feet long, but this guy looks to be between four and five feet." I spoke about the lizard's predatory nature and diet. Meanwhile, the star of the show flicked his forked tongue in and out. After we got some footage, I put the huge lizard down, and Steve leaned his head into the camera frame to have a last word.

"And they've also got teeth like a tiger shark, mate," he said with relish. "They can tear you to ribbons!"

"Thanks a lot," I said, laughing, after John stopped filming. "You should have told me that before I picked the bloody thing up!"

It was a brave new world that I found myself in. At night I would hear the sounds of the fruit bats as they came into the trees. Also in the mix were the strange, far-off grunts of the koalas as they sang out their mating calls. Herds of wild pigs passed right behind the tent. Venturing outside in the middle of the night with my dunny roll to go use a bush was a daunting experience.

Steve was a natural in front of the camera. John had to give him only one important piece of advice.

"Stevo," John instructed, "there are three people in this documentary. There's you,

Terri, and the camera. Treat the camera just like another person."

Steve's energy and enthusiasm took over. He completely relaxed, and he managed to just be himself—which was true of his entire career.

This wasn't just a film trip, it was also our honeymoon. Steve would sometimes escape the camera crew and take us up a tributary to be alone. We watched the fireflies come out. I'd never seen fireflies in Oregon. The magical little insects glowed everywhere, in the bushes and in the air. The darker it got, the brighter their blue lights burned on and off.

I had arrived in a fairyland.

Mostly, though, we worked. The tides were so huge that going out at high tide meant an easy boat ride down the river. After a full day of setting traps, checking traps, and looking for crocs, we headed back to camp late in the afternoon, at low tide. Suddenly we couldn't all ride in the boat.

Steve and I were the first ones out. As we maneuvered John Stainton and the ever-valuable camera up the river in the boat, we walked carefully along the rocky bottom.

We often encountered sinkholes and had to hang on to the side of the boat, hoping there wasn't a crocodile lying in wait down below. When we got back to camp, John had to get out of the boat and struggle through knee-deep mangrove mud. Not exactly his cup of tea, but to his credit, he never complained.

To successfully trap crocs, meat was needed for bait. This was where Sui came into her own, rounding up pigs. Feral pigs are not native to Australia but were introduced when Europeans first arrived. They root up native vegetation and raid freshwater crocodile nests, feeding on everything from plants to turtles.

Steve caught the feral pigs and kept them in makeshift corrals until he needed them. Over the years, he and Sui had become the ultimate pig-catching team. It was an amazing process to watch. Since there was no way to store large increments of fresh meat, we were off to some local cane fields at first light to catch pigs.

The cane fields were dangerous. Taipans, the third most venomous snake on earth, followed rats into the cane. As we crashed through, intent on catching pigs, it was impossible to scan the ground for snakes, so we did our best to move quickly.

At first we moved stealthily through the bush. Steve signaled to me by pointing to his nose that he could smell pigs. Sniffing the air, I caught a heavy, musky odor. We soon saw tracks and heard the rustling of bushes up ahead. Sui became absolutely frantic. She danced in place and almost jumped out of her skin. This was what she was all about.

Steve whispered, "Up front, Sui." She exploded forward, disappearing in the thick cane. Steve was right behind her. Suddenly I heard crashing sounds all around me. I realized the pigs had doubled back. Steve was yelling something, but I couldn't hear him.

A large boar burst through the bush right in front of me. Sui and Steve came up quickly behind. The big boar decided that it was time to turn and fight. Sui started yapping at the pig, dancing right in front of its nose. The boar's tusks stuck out at odd angles. It slashed at Sui, who moved like a boxer in the ring, weaving in and out, deftly maneuvering the pig so that it couldn't run and wouldn't be able to connect with those killer tusks.

Steve was on the pig in a flash. He grabbed it by the back legs, lifted it up wheelbarrow-style, and rolled it on its side. Sui was beside herself with joy, dashing in and out, her barking shrill and excited. The pig that Steve had so quickly overturned clearly weighed more than he did.

"Come over here quick," he said.

I thought, *There is no way I am going to be able to hold that pig down.* Instead, Steve directed me to grab Sui. Mission accomplished.

Day after day, Steve checked the traps for the big croc. Now it was a waiting game.

The Cattle Creek ecosystem teemed with life. It was a favorite spot for fishermen, because wherever you have crocs, you have a healthy fish population. Crocs manage a river system by culling out everything that shouldn't be there: animals that are weak, old, sick, or young. The crocs get them first. The catfish that had been introduced to Cattle Creek, for example, are much slower swimming than the native barramundi, so the catfish would be eaten first.

There was plenty of wildlife to film: water

pythons, venomous snakes, numerous beautiful birds, koalas, possums, and all kinds of lizards. But the big croc remained elusive.

Finally we found him. But something was wrong. As we approached, he failed to submerge. We were horrified to discover that the poachers had beaten us—and shot him. It was likely that he had been killed some time ago. Crocs often take a long while to die. They have the astonishing ability to shut off blood supply to an injured part of their body. The big croc had shut down and gone to the bottom of the river, at last, to succumb to his wound. He was huge, some fifteen feet long, fat and in good shape.

Steve was beside himself; he felt as if the croc's death was a personal failure. We filmed the croc and talked about what had happened. But eventually, Steve simply had to walk away. When I went to him, there were tears in his eyes. Steve had a genuine love for crocodiles and appreciated each individual animal. This croc could have been fifty years old, with mates, a family, and a history as king of this river. His death wasn't abstract to Steve. It was personal, as though he had lost a friend, and it fueled his anger toward the poacher who had killed such a magnificent animal.

Steve knew there was another croc in the area that was also in potential danger. “Maybe if we save that one,” Steve said, with resolve, “we can salvage something out of this trip.”

He didn’t give up. That night we cruised Cattle Creek again to film the trap sites. It seemed that wherever we went, Steve had an uncanny ability as a wildlife magnet. As we traveled downstream in the boat, he spotted a large carpet python on an overhanging limb.

We filmed as Steve held on to the python’s tree limb, keeping the boat steady. He talked about the snake, and how it might have been in that tree to hunt fruit bats. Suddenly the tree limb snapped, and both the branch and snake crashed down into the boat.

Everyone reacted, startled. I had been standing up, and I fell backward into the river.

Splashing to the surface would only catch a crocodile’s attention, so I let myself sink and then gradually drift up to the surface again. As my head broke the surface, I could see the boat had drifted off. I can remember looking up from the murky water and seeing the spotlight get smaller and smaller. *Don't panic,* I told myself, knowing we were right in front of a baited croc trap. I was trying to tread water without making any splashing or "hurt animal"–type movements that would attract a crocodile. I could feel my heart pounding. It was hard to breathe. I was absolutely fighting the panic.

Steve and the film crew were wrangling branch and snake. The boat motor had quit. Steve frantically attempted to start it. I could hear him swearing in the darkness. The crew member holding the spotlight divided his attention between making sure I was okay and helping Steve see what he was doing. The boat continued to drift farther and farther down the river.

Just be as motionless as possible, I told myself. I had my teeth clenched in anticipation of feeling a croc's immense jaw pressure close around my leg.

Suddenly I heard the engine roar back to life. Steve swung the boat around and gunned it. As soon as he got to me, he dragged me back in. I felt a little sick. I lay there for a moment, but the drama was not over.

Our cameraman was deathly afraid of snakes, and the carpet python was still in the bottom of the boat. Steve scooped it up. The snake decided it didn't appreciate the whole ordeal. It swung around and proceeded to grab Steve repeatedly on the forearm, bite after bite after bite.

Looking back at the footage now, the whole ordeal seems a bit amusing.

"Ah! Ah! Ah!" a male voice yells. You think it might be Steve, as he is the one being bitten, but actually it was John Stainton. He cries out in sympathy each time the python sinks its teeth into Steve's arm.

It sounds as though Steve himself is being terribly injured, when in fact the little tiny pinpricks from the carpet python's hundreds of teeth were only minor wounds. Although the teeth go deep into the flesh and it bleeds quite readily, there was no permanent scarring, no venom, and no infection.

"Are you okay, babe?" Steve asked. I told him I was. Shaken, but in one piece. Steve was okay, the python was okay, and even the cameraman seemed to have recovered. We returned the snake to its tree.

"We might as well go back to camp," Steve said, mock-sternly. "Thanks to you, we probably won't catch that croc tonight. You probably scared the living daylights out of him, landing in the water like that."

That night, lying exhausted in my swag, covered with salt water and river mud, I had a single thought running through my mind over and over. *Thank God that Steve was there.* Wherever I was in the Australian bush, whatever I was doing, I resolved that Steve had to be with me. I felt that as long as he was there, no matter what accident or incident happened, I knew I would be fine.

It wasn't just that I knew Steve would protect me and that his knowledge of the bush was so complete. I was beginning to sense something we would both come to feel and talk about seriously. When we were together, nothing bad would happen. Apart, we might be vulnerable. It was hard to explain, but it was as if the universe had brought us together and now we were as one. Whatever it was, we both felt it.

The next morning I would learn just how lucky I was to have Steve with me the night before, adrift in croc water.

* * * *

Steve got up before me and left to check the trap. The fire was already going when I crawled out of my swag. I relived the events of the night before over my cup of tea.

I heard the boat motor and saw that Steve was coming back, so I got up and ran down to the riverbank to meet him.

"We got one," he said, breathless. "A croc went in that trap after all, mate."

"I guess maybe my splashing around attracted it," I said with a grin.

He laughed. Then he turned and yelled up to the guys, "Cooee!" The whole camp erupted into action. The film crew grabbed their gear, and we went to rescue the crocodile before a poacher's bullet could claim it.

I didn't know what to expect. I had heard stories of Steve catching crocodiles. I'd seen photographs and some of his video footage. Steve took me into the crocodile enclosures at the zoo. But this was something I'd never experienced. This was in the wild.

As we approached the trap, the crocodile heard the boat motor and started thrashing. In the dim, early-morning light, all I could see was the net moving violently back and forth, a large, muddy-colored croc caught within. It was a magnificent animal. Not as big as the last crocodile, but a lumpy, bumpy dinosaur all the same.

Steve had secured the trap to a tree. The crocodile was cinched up inside, since the mouth of the trap drew shut when the weight bag dropped. Steve needed to secure the weight bag separately and get the trap stabilized, while still avoiding those jaws.

I watched him work. He retied several knots in quick succession. Once he was satisfied that it was safe, he could take into consideration the film crew and me. He explained to me what we were going to do. The object would be to get the crocodile out of the trap. We needed it completely unencumbered to be able to move it to a new location.

The mesh trap was tangled in the croc's teeth and claws. We needed to carefully untangle it. As we approached the croc, my adrenaline surged. I could feel my fingertips tingling, and my mouth went dry.

Steve positioned the camera crew so they could have the best vantage point without risk of getting nailed. Then he turned to me.

"Right," he said. "You jump on its head and I'll get the net off."

Um . . . what? I thought surely I'd misunderstood.

"Right," Steve shouted. "Now!"

So I jumped on the crocodile's head.

I lay down as flat as possible and flung my arms around its head. The croc struggled. As it swung around with me on top, I hung on for dear life, hoping I wouldn't feel those teeth on my arms. I was finally able to pin down its head.

Steve began at the tail end, rolling the trawler mesh back, working the net under the croc's massive tail. Half a crocodile's body length is taken up by its tail. Steve slipped one back leg out of the net, then another. He pushed the mesh up farther, now working directly underneath me.

I slid from one side of the crocodile to the other, always keeping my arms around the head so the croc couldn't swing around and nail Steve. As we worked, the sweat dripped off my face, as well as all the bug spray I had on. The mozzies feasted, but I hardly noticed.

My heart pounded. The crocodile would relax, but then I would feel it tense like a horse about to buck, and then my world would explode into wild thrashing, with the croc trying to shake me off. I hung on as tightly as possible.

I pressed my cheek against the top of the croc's head and got a close-up view of the head shields and calcium deposits on top of its skull. The croc would exhale, and I felt its warm, odorless breath blowing up into my bangs, brushing across my face. I felt so special as I closed my eyes to experience each breath. I was beginning to understand Steve's spiritual connection with these ancient reptiles.

Every once in a while, the crocodile would let out a guttural growl. Even though its jaws were partially held by the mesh, it was daunting to be in such close proximity to three thousand pounds per square inch of jaw pressure.

Steve gathered the mesh of the trap around the crocodile's head. This was the most dangerous part. He traded places with me and worked his hands under the net, wrapping his hands around the croc's jaws as he eased its head out of the trap.

The croc was free, with only Steve's hands clamping shut its jaws. We bound its snout and slipped on a blindfold to settle it down. Next, we determined that it was a female and measured her. She wasn't even ten feet long, but when I was lying on top of her, it felt like I was holding down a dragon.

Crocodiles have been on the planet for some sixty-five million years, looking just about like this one. They've evolved to be the most complex apex predator in their environment. They have a life expectancy similar to ours, and their physiology is surprisingly similar to ours as well: the same basic type of four-chambered heart, and a cerebral cortex. I marveled at the sixty-four long, very sharp, peg-like teeth. Here was an animal able to capture and kill animals much larger than itself.

How ironic, I thought, *that this-top-of-the-food-chain animal needs our help.*

As we motored up the river, I restrained the croc on the floor of the boat. I could feel Steve's reverence for her. He didn't just like crocodiles. He loved them.

We finally came to a good release location. We got the crocodile out onto a sandbar and slipped the ropes and blindfolds and trappings off her. She scuttled back into the water.

"She'll be afraid of boats from now on," Steve said. "She'll never get caught again. She'll have a good, healthy fear of humans, too. It'll help keep her alive."

Forever afterward, Steve and I referred to the Cattle Creek rescue as our honeymoon trip. It also marked the beginning of Steve's filming career. He was gifted with the ability to hunt down wildlife. But he hunted animals to save them, not kill them.

That's how the Crocodile Hunter was born.

CHAPTER SIX

Zoo

In spite of the death of the big croc, I felt that our time at Cattle Creek had been superb. Even before we got back to the zoo and saw the footage, there was a hint in the air that something special had been accomplished.

We were elated at saving one crocodile and bitterly disappointed at the one that had been shot. Perhaps Steve felt the failure to save the Cattle Creek croc from poachers more strongly than I did. He was normally an action man, focused on his next project. I wasn't used to him being gloomy or fixated on mortality. But he kept asking me to promise him that I'd keep the zoo going if something happened to him.

"Promise me," he said, wanting me to say it out loud.

I solemnly promised him that I would keep the zoo going. "But nothing's going to happen," I said lightly, "because the secret to being a great conservationist is living a long time."

On the drive back to the zoo, we had talked for a long time, a marathon conversation. We didn't know whether our Cattle Creek documentary would make a huge difference or not. But we agreed that through our zoo and our shared life together, we would try to change the world.

I told him about my days working at the vet hospital in Oregon, and the times I'd sit on the floor and weep, I'd be so overwhelmed by the pain and suffering visited upon innocent animals. But that burden seemed much easier to bear now, because I had someone to share it with. Steve truly understood how I felt. And I was someone who could sympathize with the depth of his dedication to wildlife.

There was a big wide world out there. We were just a small wildlife park in Australia. It was absurd to think the two of us could change the world. But our love seemed to make the impossible appear not only possible, but inevitable.

I look back on the talk we had during the ride to the zoo from Cattle Creek as helping to create the basis of our marriage. No matter what problems came along, we were determined to stay together, because side by side we could face anything.

Back at the zoo, while the documentary was being edited and before it was aired on Australian television, our sense of purpose became more firmly settled than ever. We officially took over stewardship of the zoo from Lyn and Bob, Steve's parents, who had founded it in 1970 as the Beerwah Reptile Park. We wanted to make them proud.

The new name would be simply Australia Zoo. We would build and expand. We wanted to increase viewing access to the croc enclosures so more people could see and appreciate these wonderful animals. We had grand plans.

We worked to make ends meet. We judged it a good Sunday if we had one hundred visitors, perhaps six hundred and fifty dollars in gross receipts. But running a business isn't just monitoring income, balancing the books, and ensuring quality. Part of any businessperson's plan has to include a vision for the future. Steve could look at an open, weed-choked field and see gardens, walkways, new environments for animals. His mind buzzed with projects.

It takes vision, and hard work. I would watch Steve planting trees, moving earth, and landscaping. He milled his own timber to build enclosures. He worked from dawn until well after dark, when he rigged spotlights to be able to keep working. I had never seen anything like it. He was a machine. He would go past human endurance. Often I'd catch him throwing up behind a tree out of sheer physical exhaustion.

"Don't worry about it. I just drank too much tea this morning," he said after one such incident, when I expressed my concern. He continued with the job.

Running a zoo meant being able to work with wildlife, yes. But I discovered there was so much more to it. Steve had an apprenticeship in diesel fitting, so he could operate and repair the backhoes, vehicles, and machines necessary to run the zoo. He laid brick and concrete, designed enclosures, and had an eye like an interior decorator for the end result of all his work. It didn't just have to be sturdy and well-built. It had to look good, too.

Over the course of several years in the early 1990s, I helped as Steve developed and expanded the zoo. Funds were limited. Steve did much of the work himself, making what little money we had stretch that much further. He wouldn't even have one project finished and would already be dreaming up visions of another.

It seemed like there weren't enough hours in the day, no matter how hard we worked. Luckily, we had at the zoo an amazing creature that would always give us an instant reality check, putting all our ambitions in perspective.

Harriet was a giant Galapagos land tortoise. She fascinated me. The original story was that she had been brought to Australia by whalers. Given the fact that whalers used these gentle creatures as food on long ocean voyages, Steve and I both considered this story highly unlikely. But how else could Harriet have wound up here?

We tracked her story with tortoise expert Scott Thomson, piecing together an amazing biography that would never be conclusively proved but was eminently plausible.

We believed Harriet had been collected in 1835 by Charles Darwin himself. She was brought to Australia from England in 1841 by Captain Wickham aboard the HMS *Beagle*. Actually, three giant Galapagos tortoises had been donated to the Brisbane Botanic Gardens, after Darwin realized they did not flourish in England, where he had originally taken them in 1835.

How could we determine whether Harriet was one of the Darwin Three? Scott Thomson found a giant tortoise in the collection of the Queensland Museum that had been mislabeled an Aldabran tortoise. Carved on the carapace was the animal's name, "Tom," and "1929." We now had potentially found two of the three Darwin tortoises. Harriet and Tom had been seen together in living memory. The third tortoise was never found and was presumed buried somewhere in the botanic gardens. Harriet lived on.

Steve and I became very excited at this news. Our studies and research into Harriet's history continued for years, and it was amazing to learn what a special resident we had at the zoo.

Despite her impressive background, Harriet remained attractively modest. She had a sweet personality like a little dog. She loved hibiscus flowers, and certain veggies were her favorites. Steve carried on a practice that his parents had implemented: Whatever you feed animals should be good enough for you to eat. Thus Harriet got the most beautiful mustard greens, kale, eggplant, zucchinis, and even roses.

In return, Harriet gave zoo visitors a rare chance to watch her keepers cuddle and scratch one of the grandest creatures on earth. She was the oldest living chelonian and the only living creature to have met Charles Darwin and traveled aboard the *Beagle*. And she gave us all something else, too—a lesson in how to live a long life. Don't worry too much. Take it easy. Stop and munch the flowers.

It was a lesson Steve noted and understood but could never quite take to heart. He was a meteor. Harriet was more of a mountain. In this world, we need both.

Meanwhile, I was still an out-of-her-element novice from Oregon. Steve wanted to help me feel as comfortable with snakes as I was with my mammal friends. I'd had some experience with reptiles before, but it certainly wasn't my forte. Since I was living every day with about a hundred and fifty snakes, in a country that was home to the top eleven most venomous snakes in the world, it was time for a Stevo snake education.

He knew just the right teacher. "Let me introduce you to Rosie," Steve said to me one day, bringing out a beautiful boa constrictor. She was eight feet long, as fat as my arm, and very sweet. But when I first met her, I was a bit more nervous than I wanted to admit.

"The first step is to get to know each other," Steve explained.

I tried. While Steve cooked dinner, I sat at one end of the sofa. Rosie lay coiled at the other. I eyed her suspiciously. She eyed me the same way, both of us hoping that we each didn't just suddenly fling ourselves at the other in attack. I was worried about her, and she must have been worried about me, too. Friend or foe? Back when we first met, neither of us knew.

Finally there came a revelation. I watched her, curled up on her end of the sofa, and I realized Rosie was actually more wary of me than I was of her. That's when I started to understand the thought process of the snake. Snakes are very logical: *If it's bigger than me, I'm afraid of it. If it's smaller than me, I will eat it.* Fortunately, I was way too big for Rosie to think of me as a snack.

I inched closer to her. Rosie tentatively stretched her neck out, flicked her tongue a few times, and slid into my lap. It was a monumental moment and a huge new experience for me. We began to check each other out. I stroked her soft, smooth skin. She smelled every little bit of me, and since snakes smell with their tongues, this meant a lot of flicking and licking. She licked down the front of my knee and flicked her tongue at my shoelaces. After a long day traipsing around the zoo, my shoes must have smelled . . . interesting.

Up she came. As she approached my face, I felt myself instinctively recoil. Incredibly, even though I betrayed none of my inner thoughts, Rosie seemed to sense my anxiety. She slowed down and hesitated. As I relaxed, she relaxed.

As time went by, I was able to tolerate Rosie around my shoulders. Soon I did the dishes with Rosie around my neck, and paperwork with her stretched out on the table.

We began doing most of my household chores together. She preferred small indoor spaces where she felt secure, but she became braver and braver as she trusted me more.

Before I met Rosie, I'd believed that a snake's personality was rather like that of a goldfish. But Rosie enjoyed exploring. She stretched her head out and flicked her tongue at anything I showed her. Soon she was meeting visitors at the zoo. Children derived the most delight from this. Some adults had their barriers and their suspicions about wildlife, but most children were very receptive. They would laugh as Rosie's forked tongue tickled their cheeks or touched their hair.

Rosie soon became my best friend and my favorite snake. I could always use her as a therapist, to help people with a snake phobia get over their fear. She had excellent camera presence and was a director's dream: She'd park herself on a tree limb and just stay there. Most important for the zoo, Rosie was absolutely bulletproof with children. During the course of a busy day, she often had kids lying in her coils, each one without worry or fear.

Rosie became a great snake ambassador at the zoo, and I became a convert to the wonderful world of snakes. It would not have mattered what herpetological books I read or what lectures I attended. I would never have developed a relationship with Rosie if Steve hadn't encouraged me to sit down and have dinner with her one night.

I grew to love her so much, it was all the more difficult for me when one day I let her down.

I had set her on the floor while I cleaned out her enclosure, but then I got distracted by a phone call. When I turned back around, Rosie had vanished. I looked everywhere. She was not in the living room, not in the kitchen, not down the hall. I felt panic well up within me. *There's a boa constrictor on the loose and I can't find her!* As I turned the corner and looked in the bathroom, I saw the dark maroon tip of her tail poking out from the vanity unit.

I couldn't believe what she had done. Rosie had managed to weave her body through all the drawers of the bathroom's vanity unit, wedging herself completely tight inside of it. I could not budge her. She had jammed herself in.

I screwed up all my courage, found Steve, and explained what had happened.

"What?" he exclaimed, upset. "You can't take your eyes off a snake for a second!" He examined the situation in the bathroom. His first concern was for the safety of the snake. He tried to work the drawers out of the vanity unit, but to no avail. Finally he simply tore the unit apart bare-handed.

The smaller the pieces of the unit became, the smaller I felt. Snakes have no ears, so they pick up vibrations instead. Tearing apart the vanity must have scared Rosie to death. We finally eased her out of the completely smashed unit, and I got her back in her enclosure. Steve headed back out to work. I sat down with my pile of rubble, where the sink once stood.

Through Rosie's ambassadorship, I was able to participate more in the hands-on running of the zoo. Steve gave me my own area to work in. I had baby crocodiles (saltwater and freshwater both) and lots of lizards. It was wintertime when I first took over their care. I had to be careful about feeding them. If baby crocs ate too much and it wasn't warm enough, they wouldn't be able to digest their food. All reptiles rely on the temperature of their surroundings to regulate their bodily functions. They can't heat their own bodies as mammals do. I had to crank up the heaters in their rooms, keep their tubs clean, and monitor them closely.

In addition to the crocodile babies, I also had spectacular lizards in my care: perenties, Mertens' water monitors, mangrove monitors, and lace goannas. Part of the walls of the room they were in folded out in order to expose the lizards to natural sunlight.

"Make sure they don't have any newspaper in with them," Steve said. "They'll hide under it, won't get any sun, and get too cold." Getting too hot was also a potential problem. Out in the bush, a lizard could sit on a rock virtually all day in the sun and be "fine as frog's hair," as Steve would say. The same lizard in an enclosure could not last in ten minutes in the sun. They needed to be able to thermoregulate themselves.

A consistent theme of operating the zoo was money management. Although we were in the subtropics, it did get cool in winter. Finances were tight. We couldn't afford the specific type of several-hundred-dollar heater we needed to keep the animals warm. I remember the triumph we felt when we located two kerosene heaters for only eighty-five dollars. They held enough fuel to burn twelve hours, so we were able to keep the baby crocodiles and lizards at comfortable temperatures.

I was the one-woman marketing department for the zoo. My budget was twelve hundred dollars for the whole year. I often fielded complaints from tourism board representatives, who considered me awfully cheap when I couldn't come up with fifty dollars for an advertisement in a local newspaper. Money was just that scarce.

There was no e-mail or fax machine. Everything had to be done by phone. Steve didn't even own a typewriter. Personal computer? No such thing. Filing system? No way. The Irwins had a simple but effective tool for keeping track of zoo business: a calendar diary. I used a calculator to do payroll and instituted a file-card system for keeping track of people with whom we did business.

Life was simpler then. Steve's sister Mandy worked with us, and in addition we employed three full-time staffers and one part-time staffer. That was the whole zoo crew.

My learning curve was steep not only at the zoo but around the house, too. The simplest routines back home in Oregon were totally different in the subtropics. For example, I couldn't load the dishwasher and leave it to sit, because we would end up with a house full of ants. If I left a light on in the bathroom at night, insects would somehow get in from outside and fly across the room whenever anyone entered.

I kept a wary eye on the large huntsman spiders, which grew as big as your hand. It took me a long time to get my mind around the fact that Steve wasn't going to come running every time I saw a spider or a big bug. After a while I figured out that there was really nothing from which he needed to save me. Neither the strange insects nor the spiders were dangerous.

In fact, eventually one of the giant spiders would eat one of the giant cockroaches. The subtropics featured great indoor ecosystems, as well as outdoor ones.

Steve always patiently explained to me that the giant huntsman spiders rarely bit humans. One night he had the opportunity to prove himself wrong. He rolled over one in his sleep, and the next morning he had a bruise and two little fang marks on his body. He was most concerned because of the specific location of the bite. I gleefully explained to anyone who would listen that Steve had this giant spider-bite bruise on a part of his anatomy that "will remain undisclosed."

That story made the rounds for a long time.

As precious as our money was, I had two holes into which I poured quite a lot of it. Their names were Shasta and Malina. I was determined to bring my two best animal friends from Oregon and make them part of my new life at the zoo. I missed them dearly.

No fax, no e-mail, only international long distance. The process was not easy.

I made the appropriate contacts with the Australasian Regional Association of Zoological Parks and Aquaria (ARAZPA). I also initiated the paperwork for the various government department approvals, in order to bring Malina to the zoo.

I had been working to bring my dog Shasta to Australia too. Time, effort, and money went into vet checks, special transportation boxes, a four-month quarantine in Hawaii, and a five-month one in Sydney. Quarantine worked out to twenty-six dollars a day. All of our savings were consumed in the effort to bring my dog over. Steve loved Sui so much that he understood completely why it was worth it to me.

The process took forever, and I spent my days tangled in red tape. I despaired. I loved my life and I loved the zoo, but there were times during that desperate first winter when it seemed we were fighting a losing battle.

Then our documentaries started to air on Australian television. The first one, on the Cattle Creek croc rescue, caused a minor stir. There was more interest in the zoo, and more excitement about Steve as a personality. We hurried to do more films with John Stainton. As those hit the airwaves, it felt like a slow-motion thunderclap. Croc Hunter fever began to take hold.

The shows did well in Sydney, even better in Melbourne, and absolutely fabulous in Brisbane, where they beat out a long-running number one show, the first program to do so. I believe we struck a chord among

Australians because Steve wasn't a manufactured TV personality. He actually did head out into the bush to catch crocodiles. He ran a zoo. He wore khakis. Among all the people of the world, Australians have a fine sense of the genuine. Steve was the real deal.

Although the first documentary was popular and we were continuing to film more, it would be years before we would see any financial gain from our film work. But Steve sat down with me one evening to talk about what we would do if all our grand plans ever came to fruition.

"When we start to make a quid out of Crocodile Hunter," he said, "we need to have a plan."

That evening, we made an agreement that would form the foundation of our marriage in regard to our working life together. Any money we made out of Crocodile Hunter—whether it was through documentaries, toys, or T-shirts (we barely dared to imagine that our future would hold spin-offs such as books and movies)—would go right back into conservation. We would earn a wage from working at the zoo like everybody else. But everything we earned outside of it would go toward helping wildlife, 100 percent. That was our deal.

As a result of the documentaries, our zoo business turned from a trickle to a steady stream. Only months earlier, a big day to us might have been $650 in total receipts. When we did $3,500 worth of business one Sunday, and then the next Sunday upped that record to bring in $4,500, we knew our little business was taking off.

Things were going so well that it was a total shock when I received a stern notice from the Australian immigration authorities. Suddenly it appeared that not only was it going to be a challenge to bring Shasta and Malina to my new home of Australia, I was encountering problems with my own immigration too.

Just when Steve and I had made our first tentative steps to build a wonderful life together, it looked as though it could all come tumbling down.

CHAPTER SEVEN

Stacks of Fun

Using typical bureaucratic logic, the Australian Consulate in San Francisco had informed me that it would not process my application for permanent residency in Australia unless I was residing in the United States. It wasn't enough that I had married an Australian, or that I had a full-time job and wouldn't be a drag on the economy.

I had to leave to be able to stay.

But before I went back to the States, we had the opportunity to continue filming, shooting scenes for the documentary *The Crocodile Hunter Goes West*. We packed up the truck and headed for Windorah, on the edge of the Simpson Desert. Steve's parents, Bob and Lyn, came with us, as well as

John Stainton and his crew, including Henry, the cameraman.

Steve did most of the driving. On the twenty-four-hour trip out, I took the wheel for maybe three hours total. We had a flat tire and found ourselves paying two hundred dollars to get it fixed in Quilpie, on the edge of spinifex country. Waiting to get back up and running would seem to be dead time, but there wasn't any such thing when Steve was around.

The long, spiky spinifex harbored an immense variety of animal life. In among the grass were finger-sized burrow holes in the ground. I didn't know what made them. Steve recognized them as the homes of bird-eating spiders.

I was impressed. "There are spiders that eat birds?"

"Sure thing, mate," he said. "Birds, lizards, any little thing they can get their fangs into."

He wrangled two of them out of their underground homes, and I was able to get a close-up look at them. They looked like tarantulas, only their abdomens were much larger. They rarely encountered humans, and so the two Steve handled got all fired up. I could see the venom drip from their fangs.

"These little beauties are being collected by the pet trade," Steve said, gently handling one of the giant spiders. "But they don't handle captivity well, so a lot of them die."

Henry filmed the whole episode. "When collectors dig up these beautiful spiders," Steve explained to the camera, "they often destroy their underground homes and completely ruin an entire habitat."

It was the kind of situation that always made Steve sad. He set the big girl down to return to her burrow. "Crikey," he said, "wasn't she gorgeous?"

I myself had never really considered using the words "gorgeous" and "spider" in a sentence together. After getting to know the bird-eaters, I finally settled on my own description: "cool." In their burrows, we found the remnants of their love lives. After a female met a male spider and had a passionate night of romance, she would kill and eat him.

The spiders fed by sensing vibrations on the surface. They'd emerge from their burrows and strike, killing insects, lizards, rodents, even small birds. Their fangs were like hypodermic needles, and their venom killed quickly. They'd wrap their prey up and feast on its blood.

Back on the road with all four tires intact, we immediately encountered a herd of young feral pigs. With Henry scrambling after us to film, Steve and I gave chase. Steve called the little piglets "piggy banks," and as they shot off in every direction, we had to run like the wind. Steve would dive like a football hero, launching himself through the air to grab a pig. I'd try the same technique and would just look like a sick bear, flopping over on the ground. Luckily, Sui helped round them up.

Steve caught a little black-and-white-spotted piglet and explained to the camera the harm that introduced species can do to the native environment, all the while trying to talk over the squealing pig he held in his arms.

"They're feral and not native to Australia," he said. "In some places they are causing all kinds of problems."

Eventually, after running through the bush until I was exhausted, I finally managed to catch one of the piglets. I felt a great sense of accomplishment, holding the cute little pig and filming with Steve. When we were done, I set my little piglet down.

"What is that smell?" I asked.

Steve stopped and sniffed. "Ah, you won't believe it," he said, looking past me at something near the road. "Those pigs have been feeding on that carcass over there."

I looked up to see the long-dead, putrid body. The piglets had scampered happily back to their mama. Steve and I lived with the smell of death on our hands, arms, shoes, and even our hair—for days afterward.

Bob and Lyn approached. "A pair of emus, just up the road," Bob shouted.

Steve jumped into the Ute, and we were off to get a look. We spotted the two flightless birds, an adult and a subadult, but they bolted as soon as we arrived.

"Too bad," I said, watching the emus kicking up dust. "That would have been good."

"Get Henry," Steve yelled. Then he leaped from the truck and hit the ground running.

It's impossible to catch an emu. They can reach speeds of up to forty miles an hour.

Steve sprinted off and ran like the wind after the younger bird. It was huge, nearly full grown, and running like mad. I sat in the truck and watched in shock. Henry looked as stunned as I was. There was nothing he could do but put camera to shoulder and tear off after them.

"This is going to be a good laugh to watch," I said to John.

To my amazement, the three made a big circle and began to head back in the truck's direction.

"Is it just me," I said to John, "or is he gaining on it?"

With the young emu taking huge, ground-gulping strides, the dust puffing up from each footstep, and Steve in his Timberlands kicking up the dirt right behind, they came toward us. Steve lunged forward and grabbed the bird in a bear hug. He picked the emu clean up off the ground, its big, gangly legs kicking wildly.

Steve grinned from ear to ear. Henry caught his breath and tried to stop the camera from shaking. "Emus are spectacular," Steve said exuberantly. "It's the dad who raises the kids. All the mother does is deposit her eggs in a nest scraped into the ground. Then it's the father's responsibility to raise them up."

After his commentary, Steve let the emu go. As it trotted off, Henry turned to Steve and said, "I'm not sure if I got all that."

Steve immediately bolted off like a jackrabbit and ran after the emu, and I'll be darned if he didn't catch it again. Once more Steve turned to Henry and told him all about emus. Then he kissed the bird, gave it a hug, and released it a second time.

If emus tell stories around the campfire, that one had a humdinger to tell for years to come.

We got back on the road, heading west. I remember my thoughts as we ventured into the Simpson Desert. *There's nothing out here.* The landscape was flat and lifeless. Except for the occasional jump-up—a small mesa that rose twenty or thirty feet above the desert floor—it just looked like dirt, sticks, and dead trees. The Simpson Desert is one of the hottest places on earth.

But Steve brought the desert to life, pointing out lizards, echidnas, and all kinds of wildlife. He made it into a fantastic journey.

In the middle of this vast landscape were

the two of us, the only people for miles. Steve had become adept at eluding the film crew from time to time so we could be alone. There was a local cattle station about an hour-and-a-half drive from where we were filming, a small homestead in the middle of nowhere. The owners invited the whole crew over for a home-cooked meal. Steve and I stayed in the bush, and Bob and Lyn headed to one of their favorite camping spots. After having dinner, the crew couldn't locate us. They searched in the desert for a while before deciding to sleep in the car. What was an uncomfortable night for them turned out to be a brilliant night for us!

Steve made it romantic without being traditional. His idea of a beautiful evening was building a roaring campfire, watching a spectacular sunset, and cooking a curry dinner for me in a camp oven. Then we headed out spotlighting, looking for wildlife for hours on end. It was fantastic, like the ultimate Easter egg hunt. I never knew what we'd find.

When Steve did discover something that night—the tracks of a huge goanna, or a tiny gecko hiding under a bush—he reveled in his discovery. His excitement was contagious, and I couldn't help but become excited too.

The best times in my life were out in the bush with Steve.

In the morning, the crew remained M.I.A.

"Are they going to be all right?" I asked Steve.

"They're all together and they've got a vehicle," he said. "They'll be fine."

Which meant more time for us to explore. Near the camp was a man-made dam carved out of the desert. The cattle stations created these dams so that across the vast, million-acre properties, the cattle could roam freely and not have to be checked regularly. The cattle could count on these dams, as they held water from the occasional rain shower.

The wildlife knew where to get a drink as well. We crept up on the dam before sunrise. I could feel Steve's tension as we peeked over the dirt-bank lip, not knowing what we would see. This morning a family of dingoes gathered beside the water. The adults fed on a feral cat they had killed. The pups sat a few yards away, waiting their turn. Feral cats look exactly like house cats, and they looked out of place in the remote, harsh outback. The dingoes took full advantage, since they had a family to feed.

Steve and I watched the dingo family play out its drama for a long time. Then we edged our way down to the dam and hopped in. The water was cold, but it felt good.

"This is great," I said, as we swam together.

"I've been coming here since I was just a little tacker," Steve said. Bob had brought his young son with him on his research trips, studying the snakes of the region.

As I walked in and out of the water, washing up, shampooing my hair, and relishing the chance to clean off some of the desert dust, I noticed something hard underfoot.

"Steve, I stepped on something here," I said.

He immediately started clearing the bottom of the pond, tugging on what I had felt beneath the murky water.

"Tree limb," I guessed.

"Look around," Steve said, yanking at the mired object. "No trees here at all."

He couldn't budge whatever it was, but he didn't give up. He went back to camp, drove to the dam in his Ute, and tied a chain to the obstacle. As he backed up the truck, the chain tightened. Slowly a cow's pelvis emerged from the muck.

I watched with horror as Steve dislodged an entire cow carcass that had been decomposing right where I had been enjoying my refreshing dip. I must have been poking among its rib cage while I brushed my teeth and washed my hair.

Steve dragged the carcass a good distance off.

"Do you think we should tell the crew?" he asked me when he came back.

"Maybe what they don't know won't hurt them," I said.

Steve nodded. "They probably won't brush their teeth in there, anyway."

"Probably not," I said, pondering the possibility of future romantic dips with Steve, and what might lurk under the water at the next dam.

When we returned to camp, Steve insisted I sit down and not lift a finger while he cooked me a real Aussie breakfast: bacon and sausage with eggs, and toast with Vegemite. This last treat was a pastelike spread that's an Australian tradition. For an Oregon girl, it was a hard sell. I always thought Vegemite tasted like a salty B vitamin. I chowed down, though, determined to learn to love it.

As the sun rose in full, Steve began to get bored. He was antsy. He wanted to go wrangle something, discover something, film anything. Finally, at midmorning, the crew showed up.

"Let's go," Steve said. "There's an eagle's nest my dad showed me when I was just a billy lid. I want to see if it might still be there."

Right, I thought, *a nest you saw with Bob years ago. What are the chances we're going to find* that?

John looked longingly at the dam. "Thought we might have a tub first," he said. The grime of the desert covered all of them.

"Oh, I think we should go," I said hastily, the cow carcass fresh in my mind. "You don't need a bath, do you, guys?"

"Come on," Steve urged. "Wedge-tailed eagles!"

No rest for the weary.

"So, Steve," I said as gently as I could, not wanting to dissuade him as we headed out. "How old were you when Bob took you to see this nest?"

"Must've been six," he said. More than two decades ago. I stared around at the limitless horizon. I had my doubts. I watched Steve's eyes dart across the landscape. He struck out in a particular direction and led us over a series of jump-ups. Then he'd get his bearings and head off again.

One hour. Two hours. If someone had put a gun to my head I could not have led them back to the dam.

"I think I know where it is," Steve said abruptly. We continued on a little farther. Sure enough, in the distance I saw an unusually large eucalypt. In its main fork was what appeared to be a thick pile of debris and sticks, carefully laid together, that must have been eight feet thick.

There it was, an eagle's nest, twenty feet off the ground.

As we approached, we could see the tip of a bird's wing hanging over the edge of the nest. I looked at Steve. He had the same thought I did: There was a dead eagle in the nest. But he swung up into the tree anyway, and after a moment called down to us, "Bring the camera up here."

Henry tried, but there was no way he could climb the tree carrying his gear. He hoisted the camera up to Steve instead. As Steve filmed, he described what he saw.

"Two eaglets," he said. "One well-developed chick and one chick that looks really bad, really tired."

That was nature's way. When times were good, both eagle chicks would fledge. But there wasn't always enough food to fledge two babies. The stronger chick would dominate at feeding time and get most of the food. Sometimes one chick would push the other out of the nest to its death, and the parents would be left to raise just one.

Times were hard out on the edge of the Simpson Desert. It looked as though only one chick would survive. As we studied the structure, we could see how it had been added to over time. The nest may have been more than one hundred years old.

As we surveyed the nest further, we discovered that it was full of bones. We used them to tell us what the chicks had been eating. As I examined the ground beneath the nest, I saw more bone fragments, littered far and wide. Almost all of them were the remains of bearded dragons. Poking up from the dirt were skulls, bits of skin, and the lizards' hard scales. Mama and Papa Wedge-tail had been flying day in and day out, hunting the big bearded dragon lizards to feed their young.

More amazing than that, though, was the fact that Steve had been able to locate the eagle's nest so many years after he'd first visited it.

We left, allowing the survival-of-the-fittest drama to play out between the chicks. They would live or die according to the harsh laws of nature. We headed deeper into the desert, to the black soil plains, after the most venomous snake on earth.

In the late 1800s, cattle musterers drove their herds across thousands of miles of the arid landscape on the edges of the Simpson Desert. In cracks and fissures in the black soil lived snakes that would emerge from their underground homes to heat up in the sun. As the cattle approached, the snakes would move—giving the drovers the impression that they were actually following the cattle.

"Whoa," said the drovers, "those are some real fierce snakes."

That's the story of how the fierce snake got its name. It is, drop for drop, more venomous than any snake in the world, but it causes little human disruption because it lives in such a remote environment. Fierce snakes disappear into subterranean holes and cracks, lying in wait for when the rat plague happens, as it does every few years. Then it's happy days for the snakes, as they eat their fill.

Not until the 1970s was the species rediscovered after first being described some eighty years earlier. Steve's dad Bob was passionate about these secretive snakes, and he joined the scientists at the Queensland Museum to study them.

Steve knew just how and when to find them. We headed out early the next morning, before there was wind. The temperature was exactly right at eighty-six degrees Fahrenheit. Steve got a faraway look in his eye, as though he was concentrating or communicating. Then he headed off. Ten minutes later, we were on the trail of a fierce snake.

"Would you like to tail one?" Steve asked.

"Are you kidding?" I said. "I don't know how to catch a fierce snake."

Steve had already "tailed" one of the snakes. Gently grabbing the end of its tail, he could hold it at arm's length and examine it. During this procedure, snakes would often defecate, and we could get some clue about what they'd been eating. Steve would tail a snake, put it in a bag, release it, and keep what remained.

"You grab the next one," Steve said. He spotted a four- or five-foot-long fierce snake. It glistened in the sun like glass, brilliantly shiny and sleek.

"It's warming up now," Steve said as we approached. "You're going to have to be quick."

Yes, Terri, I said to myself, *please be quick so as not to get struck by the most venomous snake on earth. If you get bitten out here, you're in a load of trouble.*

We crept up behind the fierce snake. I got close enough to grab it, but the snake suddenly and violently swung its head around, directly at me, poised and ready to strike. I backed off abruptly. Time and again I approached the snake just as I'd seen Steve do it: Walk up behind the snake as it started to slither away, and grab it by the tail. I knew what to do, but I couldn't do it. Every time I reached down, the snake would swing around and I would jump a mile.

We wandered farther and farther on the trail of the snake. I could see our truck way in the distance. I sweated profusely. I kept thinking the same thought. *If I get bitten by this snake, I'm dead.* Then I would try to push that thought away. *Stop thinking, just grab the snake. Steve wouldn't ask you to do something that you couldn't do.*

But the whole process was becoming ridiculous. "What am I doing wrong?" I wailed.

"You are too bloody scared," Steve said.

"Oh," I said.

Then I reached down and picked up the snake.

It was magic. Once I had the nice, soft, supple body in my hands, it was as though the snake and I had a connection. Its skin was warm to my touch from sitting in the sun. I suddenly understood exactly how to hold on so it wouldn't get away, and yet not squeeze it so tightly that it would get angry. The snake naturally kept trying to move off. I let the front part of its body stay on the ground and held the tail up.

I felt such triumph—not that I had dominated the snake, but that it had let me pick it up. Steve held out the catch bag, and I carefully dropped the snake in. He tied a knot in the bag. We looked at each other and grinned. Then we both whooped and hollered and jumped in the air. He hugged and kissed me.

"I'm proud of you, Terri," he said. Once again I marveled at Steve's instincts. He knew that this particular snake would be okay for me to pick up. He never hesitated, he never yelled at me or coached me—until I asked for help. Then he simply told me what to do.

We headed back to the zoo, and back to the tangle of my immigration red tape. I had a renewed sense of confidence. I felt if I could face fierce snakes, I could face anything, even the Australian consulate.

The lessons I took away from that trip always stayed with me. Give Steve the benefit of the doubt. If he takes off running after an emu, get the camera ready, because he'll come back with one. If he says he'll find a specific spot in a desolate landscape that he last visited more than twenty years before, don't question him. Just ask him when he thinks we'll get there.

My education was just beginning. I would soon learn a few skills that no aspiring wildlife warrior should be without.

CHAPTER EIGHT

Egg Stealing

I flew back to the States in December of 1992 with conflicting emotions. I was excited to see my family and friends. But I was sad to be away from Steve.

Part of the problem was that the process didn't seem to make any sense. First I had to show up in the States and prove I was actually present, or I would never be allowed to immigrate back to Australia. And, oh yeah, the person to whom I had to prove my presence was not, at the moment, present herself.

Checks for processing fees went missing, as did passport photos and certain signed documents. I had to obtain another set of medical exams, blood work, tuberculosis tests, and police record checks—and in response, I got lots of "maybe's" and "come back tomorrow's." It would have been funny, in a surreal sort of way, if I had not been missing Steve so much.

This was when we should have still been in our honeymoon days, not torn apart. A month stretched into six weeks. Steve and I tried keeping our love alive through long-distance calls, but I realized that Steve informing me over the phone that "our largest reticulated python died" or "the lace monitors are laying eggs" was no substitute for being with him.

It was frustrating. There was no point in sitting still and waiting, so I went back to work with the flagging business.

When my visa finally came, it had been nearly two months, and it felt like Christmas morning. That night we had a good-bye party at the restaurant my sister owned, and my whole family came. Some brought homemade cookies, others brought presents, and we had a celebration. Although I knew I would miss everyone, I was ready to go home.

Home didn't mean Oregon to me anymore. It meant, simply, by Steve's side.

When I arrived back at the zoo, we fell in

love all over again. Steve and I were inseparable. Our nights were filled with celebrating our reunion. The days were filled with running the zoo together, full speed ahead. Crowds were coming in bigger than ever before. We enjoyed yet another record-breaking day for attendance. Rehab animals poured in too: joey kangaroos, a lizard with two broken legs, an eagle knocked out by poison.

My heart was full. It felt good to be back at work. I had missed my animal friends—the kangaroos, cassowaries, and crocodiles.

Steve and I had to shift an alligator to a new enclosure, and John came to film. Working with these large crocodilians was still pretty new to me. Steve jumped in and grabbed the full-grown female alligator, which immediately started heading for the water, dragging Steve with her.

"Grab her back legs!" he called to me.

I grabbed the alligator's back leg and tail, trying to slow her down. Steve swung to the side to try to thwart her moving away. His knee twisted, and then I heard it pop. That seemingly minor event contributed to more serious knee problems that would plague

Steve unendingly. I felt terrible. If I had done a better job at holding the gator, he might not have wrenched his knee.

"Don't worry about it, babe," he told me that night. He refused to let me help ice it down. He could tell I thought it was my fault. "My knee's been giving me curry since high school."

There never seemed to be a dull moment. Steve came running into the house one morning before the zoo opened. "Throw on your robe, quick," he said. I followed Steve to the alligator enclosure and couldn't believe my eyes. Two of our adult females, known as the "Fang Sisters," had decided to battle over the same nesting spot in their enclosure. They were locked down, their teeth tearing through each other's skulls. Blood pooled on both their heads. Neither sister would let go for anything.

"Get in!" Steve shouted. "We've got to get them apart." He told me to jump one while he jumped the other. Once we had them more or less secured, he began the agonizing process of prying their jaws apart.

Mud and blood splattered over both of us. I watched Steve struggle with the dueling alligators, locked in mortal combat.

They seemed intent on killing each other, and he was intent on saving them both. All at once the girls let go, but then immediately swung back into the fight. It took both of us, with all our strength, to hold them apart.

We sat there for some time in the mud, each holding a blood-soaked alligator. We looked at each other, hanging on for grim death, knowing that if either of us let go, it would happen all over again. It was early in the morning and no one else was at the zoo. Steve had hold of one nine-foot alligator. I had the other. It seemed like an eternity that we sat there, in a stalemate.

I didn't think I could hold on much longer. Finally Steve got his arm under his alligator and swung her around. He jumped up, grabbed a fence panel, and stuck that between the two alligators to manipulate them apart. Brandishing the panel like a bullfighter's red cape, Steve kept the two alligators separated while I ran to get building materials so he could improvise a barrier. Bull alligators get along much better than the females. The females tend to fight for nesting spaces, whereas the guys simply coexist. There was no way the Fang Sisters were ever going to share nesting space.

I slowly became familiar with the personalities of all the zoo's crocodilians. They were as individual as people. I got to know them intimately during nesting season. Saltwater crocodiles deposit around sixty eggs a season. If you leave them all in the nest, some will break, and the rotten-egg smell becomes overpowering—so one of the tasks of the zoo crew was to remove the eggs.

Mary, our oldest female croc, was easy to work with because she would tear after anyone who approached, leaving her nest unprotected. Cookie was another matter. She sat directly on top of her nest and would not leave. Steve had to get in close in order to coax her away. Whenever she came off the nest to make a flying lunge at Steve, my job was to sneak in and madly grab as many eggs as I could. On my first raid, I took sixty-six eggs out of Cookie's nest.

We had to move a lot of smaller crocodiles from one enclosure to another as they were growing. The bigger crocs would become dominant over the smaller ones, and it made everything difficult, including feeding time. One day we invited John to bring his crew and film a move with some of the smaller salties. They were only about three feet long, but were still almost more than I could handle, with snapping, biting jaws and thrashing, spinning bodies. In the end, we were all covered from head to toe with mud, laughing.

The zoo crocs were stars. Mary got to appear in *Endless Summer 2,* the sequel to the legendary 1960s surfing travelogue. Since he was a boy, Steve was always a mad keen surfer. In the movie, Steve played—what else?—a surfer carrying his board past a billabong with a crocodile in it.

Mary played her part perfectly. The filmmakers set up in her enclosure. She sat showing off her lumpy, bumpy head, looking absolutely ferocious. Steve walked nonchalantly past, carrying a surfboard, his legs filmed dramatically close to Mary and her big teeth.

The thousand dollars Steve's legs earned for his cameo helped fund a wedge-tailed eagle enclosure at the zoo, a huge space with logs suspended from the roof for easy perching. As usual, Steve built it all himself. The enclosure provided a home for two injured eagles, and it was a great educational exhibit as well. We were keeping our promise to put every penny the Croc Hunter earned right back into conservation.

Around the time Steve finished the eagle enclosure, we got our first blast of bad press. An Australian program ran an "exposé" on the zoo, on our documentaries, and on Steve. There it was, on national television for all of Australia to see. Steve's wildlife work wasn't real. He was a magician, and what people saw on screen was sleight of hand.

The program cut deep for Steve, who had spent his whole life cultivating relationships with wild animals and wanted to share his passion with the world. It really hurt his feelings, and I suffered to see him suffer. The incident was a lesson in the way the world worked. The fact that people actually made up stuff for the show got to me. In the end, Steve handled it better than I did. I experienced bad dreams and felt a little sick. I never minded if people said bad things about me. I knew who I was and what I stood for. But to hear someone say something bad about Steve really cut me to the core.

Luckily, better days were just around the corner.

Shasta was barking and howling, overjoyed to see me. After unending paperwork and nine months of quarantine, she was finally arriving in Brisbane. I met her at the airport. When I first spotted her, she was growling at the air-freight personnel. As soon as she saw me, her entire expression changed. It was a magic moment.

Even though the heat clobbered her at first, Shasta took to her new home well. She had a full two acres of yard with plenty of shade, and she could come into the house whenever she wanted. It was like having a little piece of home with me again.

At that point in time, between Steve and myself, I was the cash-rich one. I had around $120,000 in the bank after selling my Oregon house and my business, Westates Flagman. We both wanted to expand the zoo and were looking at adjacent properties. A two-acre tract was up for sale, but the owners were asking $60,000 for it.

If we purchased the land, the zoo would be enlarged from four acres to six. At the time, it seemed like an enormous step to take. We argued back and forth. We talked, dreamed, and planned. Steve always seemed to worry about the future.

"If anything happens to me, promise that you'll take care of the zoo."

"Of course I will," I said. "That's easy to promise, but nothing is going to happen to you. Don't worry."

"Will you still love me if a croc grabs me and I lose an arm or a leg?"

"Yes, of course I would still love you," I said.

But there were many evenings when he would run through improbable scenarios, just checking to see how I really felt. One night he looked particularly concerned, his brow furrowed.

"What's up?" I asked.

"Tell me why you married me."

I laughed. "Because you're hot in the cot."

That broke the tension, and he laughed too. We both relaxed a little bit. But he would sometimes wonder if I'd married him just because I loved him, or if it was because he was a bit of Tarzan and Croc Dundee and Indiana Jones all rolled into one.

"I'm in love with Steve Irwin," I assured him, "and part of the reason I love you is because you are such a staunch advocate for wildlife. Your empathy and compassion for all animals is part of it too. But most of all, I know that destiny brought us together."

Steve continued our serious discussion, and he spoke of his mortality. He was convinced that he would never reach forty. That's why he was in such a hurry all the time, to get as much done as he could. He didn't feel sad about it. He only felt the motivation to make a difference before he was gone.

"I'm not afraid of death," he said. "I'm only afraid of dying. I don't want to get sick and dwindle. I love working hard and playing hard and living hard, and making every moment count."

I learned so much from Steve. He helped me reevaluate my own purpose, my own life. What would happen if I didn't make it to forty? What legacy would I leave?

That evening he was unusually contemplative. "None of our petty problems really matter," he said.

I agreed. "In a hundred years, what difference is it going to make, worrying about this two acres of land? We need to focus on the real change that will make the world a better place for our children and grandchildren."

Steve gave me a strange look. Children? We had never discussed having children much, because we were flat strapped. The thought of filming more documentaries, running the zoo, *and* raising a family was just too daunting. But that evening we did agree on one thing: We would spend some of my savings and make the leap to enlarge the zoo. We were both so happy with our decision.

"We're lucky that we met before I became the Crocodile Hunter," he said.

I knew what he was talking about. It made things a lot easier, a lot more clear-cut. I had fallen in love with Steve Irwin, not the guy on TV.

"I don't know how they do it," he said.

"Who?" I asked.

"People in the limelight," he said. "How do they tell who's in it for them and who's just after their celebrity? It puts a new slant on everything. Not for us, though," he added.

"Too right," I agreed.

Around that time, Steve managed to secure a piece of posterity in a way he never expected. While shooting a film called *Hidden River,* he and I were rowing past the camera to get a particular shot. Steve suddenly leaped to his feet and flung himself out of the boat.

He vanished beneath the water. By this time I was used to Steve bolting off for no apparent reason. I turned around to look for him, and after what seemed like a great deal of time had passed, he surfaced with something. It was big and round, like a dinner plate.

"What have you got?"

He hoisted a large, pale turtle to the surface and hauled it into the boat. It had a light-colored head, an almost pink nose, and beautiful, delicate coloring. Its watery, saucer-shaped eyes craned up and looked at Steve. *Now you've got me, what are you going to do with me?*

"Crikey, I've only ever seen this species once before, with my dad," Steve marveled. As it turned out, he had discovered a new species of turtle right there in the middle of the river. We photographed his find, filmed it, measured it, and weighed it.

The Queensland Museum verified that it was an undescribed species that would be called Irwin's turtle—*Elseya irwini,* forever named after Steve.

Back at the zoo, now that we had decided to buy the additional two acres, Steve was determined to open the whole of the original four acres to the public. The Crocodile Environmental Park had always been a separate part of the zoo, with separate admission, open only for croc shows. But now, as the crowds increased as a result of our documentaries, he wanted to showcase the crocs.

Steve planned the grand opening of the Crocodile Environmental Park for the Christmas school holidays. That meant building extra walkways, ramps, and grandstands for visibility, and erecting double fences all around the enclosures so people couldn't come in close proximity to the crocodiles. It was a tremendous amount of work.

Steve spent the spring feverishly concreting crocodile ponds. He shifted the animals around so that each croc was in a good position for viewing. He worked tirelessly. The weather didn't cooperate, and the wet season came early that year. Steve started in September and worked straight through to Christmas, nearly sixteen straight weeks of backbreaking labor.

His focus was always on the animals he loved. I knew that he didn't want people showing up at the zoo just to see him, the Crocodile Hunter. He wanted people to come to see his crocs. That's what Steve was all about. Working so hard was his way of making sure that visitors would have the best opportunity to love crocodiles like he did.

Steve ended up with terrible concrete burns on his arms and hands. His wrist had to be splinted. Through it all he never complained. We made it in time and on schedule. We opened for Christmas and the Australian school holidays, and the new layout was a huge success. The zoo visitors streamed in, and everyone was thrilled to see crocs just like they would in the wild. They left the zoo with a new appreciation for Steve's favorite animal.

Soon afterward, an effort to introduce the public to another Australian icon had us embarking on an epic journey.

CHAPTER NINE

"I Know What We Have to Do"

Steve had completed the zoo expansions to cope with the greater influx of visitors. After the school holidays, we were immediately off on a new, ambitious documentary expedition. We would trace the whole of Australia's legendary dingo fence, constructed across southeastern sheep country to keep out the predatory dingoes. Originally nearly five thousand miles long and almost four times the length of the Great Wall of China, now only about three thousand miles remained—but it was still the longest man-made structure in the world.

Steve was curious to see how the fence worked. No one was certain how effective it was. Of course, there were dingoes all over sheep country, so it wasn't clear whether the fence was really working or if dingo numbers were lowered by graziers with guns and poison bait.

Good or bad, the fence was a true Australian phenomenon. We were determined to document it as thoroughly as possible, tracing its course through some of the most remote outback on earth. Simply from a logistical point of view, the project would be a tremendous undertaking. Taking a camera crew on such a journey would be a huge responsibility for Steve—just the kind of challenge he loved.

Steve and I were looking forward to filming again with John Stainton. As our producer and director, John was very clever to let Steve do what he did best, and then edit the footage to put the final touches on the whole adventure. We worked together well and were all becoming fast friends.

John always struck me as an unlikely wildlife warrior. In all the years we worked together, I never saw him wrangle any wildlife, not even a gecko. He also managed to stay impossibly clean in spite of the adverse conditions we often found ourselves in. To his credit, he could keep up with Steve no matter how many flies, how much heat or other hardships he had to endure in the bush. But on a trip like this, there was no better filmmaker in the world.

Sui came with us, but Shasta stayed home in the shade. This trip would be just too action-packed for my aging dog. Sui, on the other hand, would have a great time, as she was used to going bush—it was like her second home. The only danger would be the 1080 poison baits that were set for the dingoes.

We started where the northern end of the fence began, in Queensland. We met the man in charge of a 1,500-mile northern section of the fence. He had a crew of twenty-three men working under him, just to keep the fence repaired and intact. We listened as he and his wife told us their wildlife stories. I wasn't sure why, but they seemed to really hate emus. I think it was because a panicked, running emu could put a hole right through the fence.

"You know, an emu is supposed to be able to run sixty kilometers per hour," he said, relishing his story. "But if I run my truck right up their bum, they will actually reach about sixty-eight kilometers an hour. It's funny how they look back over their shoulder just before they get run over."

They laughed long and loud until they realized that none of us were laughing with them. His wife must have thought we didn't get the joke, because she tried to explain it further. "Our oldest child, he always begs his dad," she told us, "'Run down an emu, Dad, run down an emu!'"

While we drove the fence line afterward, it was obvious that Steve was trying to get back to the job at hand and move on from the awkward conversation. Suddenly he had a premonition. He turned to me. "Something's going to happen," he said.

Just ahead of us, a koala ran through a paddock over open ground. Steve immediately jumped out of the truck.

"Get John and catch up!" Steve yelled.

I scrambled into the driver's seat, bouncing like hell over the muddy track, rounding up John and the crew to come film Steve's encounter with the koala.

"How did you know something was going to happen?" I asked Steve, once we'd filmed the koala and gotten it safely to a nearby tree. "How did you sense it?"

He shrugged. "I don't know, mate, it's the

strangest thing." Were Steve's bush instincts simply more finely honed than anyone else's? I didn't think it was that simple. He seemed to be able to tune into some sixth sense with wildlife. After years in the bush, he had refined his gift into an uncanny ability.

The dingo fence is not well known by all Australians. That's because you can't just drive down the fence line as if you're visiting a tourist attraction. The fence runs through private property, so permission from the landowner—and in some cases a permit—is required, primarily to protect the fence from vandals. Also, some of the areas along the fence line are incredibly remote. It's not the place for inexperienced travelers.

As we passed through the tiny community of Thargaminda, I took the rare opportunity to indulge in a hot shower at the police station, while Steve checked on road conditions. Some of the local children noticed us in town, and we were invited to make an appearance at their school. We met all fifty-one students.

"You are so lucky to have such beautiful snakes out here," Steve said. He explained how to live safely with the venomous snakes in the region, and even demonstrated first aid for snakebites. The kids were hanging on his every word.

Coming back from the school, Steve suddenly slammed on the brakes, skidding over the dirt. He cursed himself. "I was going too fast," he said. "I think I ran over a bearded dragon."

He got out of the truck, completely crestfallen, until he discovered that the lizard was alive and well, sitting poised in the middle of the road.

Steve got the lizard off the road and then lay down on the dirt with it to get it on film. "What a little ripper," he said. "Look how he pops out his beard as a defense mechanism. He's got all those spiny scales down his back to keep predators from eating him."

Steve was face-to-face with the lizard, which was all puffed up, trying to look intimidating. He was just inches away as he spoke with passion about the little desert dweller. The lizard, though, had other ideas. He decided he was a little bit tougher than Stevo. In an instant, the lizard had launched himself straight up in the air and latched onto Steve's face.

Steve jumped back, but not before he'd been solidly bitten on the nose.

"You bit me on the nose, you little brat!"

I burst out laughing. Steve took the opportunity to reiterate an important lesson. Whenever an animal nails you, it's not the animal's fault. It's your fault.

"I was sitting nose-to-nose with the little bloke," he said. "Of course he was going to bite me." He held no contempt for the lizard. Meanwhile, the crew and I were still recovering. We laughed so hard tears streamed down our faces. The lizard seemed to smile himself as he ran off and skittered up a log.

As we continued down the dingo fence, we passed through gate after gate. Steve was driving, so I was the designated "gate getter." Every single gate that we encountered had some new and inventive method of latching shut. Each farmer had his or her own design, and some were fascinatingly complicated. I'd have to look very carefully as I undid the contraption, so I'd have a hope of getting it properly closed again.

Stop the truck. Figure out the gate. Open the gate, drive the truck through, close the gate.

Some of the gates had been closed for

years and years, and the saltbush had grown up to block them. I tried to push these gigantic overgrown tumbleweeds out of the way, while Steve was ever anxious to get going. I got good at battling my way through gate after gate.

It was when we had to stop for Steve to change our second tire of the day that the unthinkable happened.

Sui ran off into the bush and grabbed what looked like a small piece of wood. She was always chewing some stick, so I didn't pay any particular attention. Then suddenly the fact of where we were hit me full blast. I ran over to her.

"Drop it," I yelled. She spat out the piece of wood, which turned out to be an ancient, dried-out piece of meat.

Signs warning against 1080 poison had been posted on almost every gate that we went through. A cruel poison, 1080 basically makes a dog go mad. It will salivate and run around frantically, seemingly in extreme pain. Finally it will foam at the mouth and go into seizure, before it collapses. It's a horrific way to die.

We were afraid that the old piece of meat had originally been dosed with 1080. We spent a fretful night, monitoring Sui. She never showed any symptoms of poisoning, so I must have gotten to her just in time.

Mile after mile, we followed the dingo fence—and didn't find a single live dingo. We kept finding dead ones, hanging from trees and fences. When a dingo is killed, it has to be scalped in a certain way to qualify for a bounty.

We saw endless dingoes skinned from their ears down their back, including their tail. The bounty hunters hang the carcass or pelt on whatever side of the fence the dingo was shot. That tells anyone who is passing by which side of the fence the dingo had been seen on. The hunters get ten dollars for each dingo scalp.

As we continued heading south through the Flinders Ranges, we encountered harsh weather. It was freezing cold, and the rain came down horizontally. We drove until almost dark. In the headlights of the truck, I saw small animals popping out of the ground everywhere.

Steve leaped out of the truck excitedly and motioned me over to get a close-up look at the creatures emerging from the mud.

"Cycloranas," Steve said, "water-holding frogs." He explained that these frogs would burrow into the ground and then cover themselves with a membrane that would hold in water. They wouldn't pee, and none of their bodily fluids would evaporate. They could remain underground for weeks, months, or even years, until the next rain hit.

"Then they emerge up from their tiny tombs, lose their membrane, and are good as gold," Steve said, marveling. "They're ready now to reproduce and feed and do their own thing."

It was an epic task to get the camera out and set up the waterproof gear to film the cycloranas. The rain finally broke, and Steve was able to film a scene. We had been driving all day, out in the rain, changing flat tires from the debris on the track. Steve even had to repair the fence when the crew's truck slid sideways across the slippery mud, knocking a neat hole in one section. Everybody was beyond exhausted.

No matter how hard Steve tried, he couldn't get his words right. He couldn't properly explain how the frogs could go so long without water. "Membranes" became "mum-branes," "water-filled" was "water-flood."

We were all getting frustrated. John said, exasperated, "Just give us something really concise." I whispered two words into Steve's ear. He turned to the camera.

"Water . . . nah," he said. The whole crew cracked up. Two words to sum up the water-holding frog.

That night there was no way to light a fire to cook dinner. We got out a loaf of bread and a container of tomato sauce, and everyone had sauce sandwiches in the car. Since the vehicles were packed full of gear, it was impossible to sleep inside. No use erecting tarps, either, in the driving, sideways rain. So Steve laid out our swags with Sui in between them, and then wrapped the tarp around us like a giant burrito. We slept like that, with the rain pelting down on top of us. But we were so completely exhausted that we slept just fine.

The next morning, the sun rose to a clear day. We all realized how muddy and road-weary we were after our eventful evening. One of the most challenging aspects of our journey was finding a place to take a tub. There weren't always dams handy, and drinking water was too precious to bathe in. But since we were traveling along the dingo fence, we were in livestock country. It wasn't unusual to come upon a trough with water running from a bore pipe, out in the middle of nowhere.

In the daylight, we were lucky enough to spot a sheep trough not far from where we'd camped. This trough didn't have a float valve, so it had overflowed and made a bit of a pond around itself. With all the sheep coming and going, the "pond" was more like thick, oozing mud than water. In spite of the obvious challenge of getting past the mud, I was determined to take advantage of a nice tub. As the only woman on the trip, I pulled the whole "ladies first" thing and headed off.

I was excited as I hiked over with my toothbrush, soap, and shampoo. But as I arrived I was greeted by the overwhelming smell—a sheep had gotten bogged down in the mud and died some time ago. Its body was partially liquefied and teeming with maggots. Ignoring this little friend would be difficult, but I had no idea when I'd get my next chance to clean up. I picked my way around the mud and balanced precariously on the edge of the concrete slab that the trough rested on. The water was dribbling in slowly from the bore pipe, and three-quarters of the surface of the water was covered in an algae-like slime.

After removing a patch of the green goo, I stashed my clothes on a dry corner of the concrete and eased myself in. I tried not to think about the water bugs nibbling on me, and I made a real effort not to stir up the sludge on the bottom of the trough—remnants of dead birds that had drowned. *Put it out of your mind,* I thought.

As I held my breath, I went under. I resolved that I wouldn't wash my hair again for a week. It was so icky to stick my head clear under! I finished up and let everyone have their turn. I suppose it was better than not bathing at all . . . perhaps.

We spent twenty days and endured three thousand miles of jolting, pounding, off-road bush driving. But we had a hard-won sense of accomplishment when we pulled up on the stunning cliff-side view of the Great Australian Bight, a huge open bay carved out of the southern coastline. We had made it.

Below us, three hundred feet down a sheer rock face, was the Southern Ocean. A pod of southern right whales passed by, their calves following along with them. Steve and I and the crew watched the family dramas of the whales play out below us.

A calf felt naughty and went darting away from his mother's side. *Come back,* the mother called, *come back, come back, you naughty little whale.* When she was under the water, we couldn't hear anything, but as she surfaced we could actually hear the whale song from our perch three hundred feet in the air.

Mama scolded the calf, and we saw the young whale come dutifully shooting back over to follow his mother for a while. Sometimes the calf would approach his mama for a drink of milk and nurse for a few minutes. Then he would escape once more, and the whole scenario played itself out all over again.

We watched the whales for hours. That night around the campfire, we discussed whaling, how sad and cruel and horrible it was.

"If we killed cows the way we killed whales, people wouldn't stand for it," Steve said. "Imagine if you drove a truck with a torpedo gun off the back. When you saw a cow you fired at it, and then you either electrocuted it over the course of half an hour or the head of the torpedo blew up inside of it, rendering it unable to walk or move until it finally bled to death."

"We've got to get that message out," I said to Steve. But his idea was to bring the beauty and joy of the whales to people, so that they would naturally fall in love with them and not want to hurt them. He didn't want to dwell on images that would make people sad and upset.

Steve remained thoughtful and silent as the fire died. The ocean sounded against the cliffs below. The games of the whale families played over and over in our minds.

In spite of our extensive searching, we never saw a live dingo down the whole line of our journey. It was time to try a different approach. The next morning the helicopter pilot arrived early. Going up with him, Steve actually finally spotted some dingoes from the air.

The beautiful, ginger-colored dogs played along the fence, jumping over it or skirting under it with effortless ease.

* * * *

School holidays were upon us, and it would be getting busy at home, so I returned to the zoo by air, while Steve drove the Ute back. Greeting Shasta after my long time away made me feel both comforted and homesick. I missed my cougar, Malina, so much, and I wanted to continue to work on protecting cougars back in the States. So I resumed my efforts to bring Malina over to Australia.

I soon learned that it is always easier for a bureaucrat to say no. They can't get in trouble saying no. While some government departments were extremely supportive, others wouldn't give me the time of day. I was absolutely crestfallen when ARAZPA would not support my application. In addition, ARAZPA's Taxon Advisory Group (TAG), an accrediting organization for zoos, was of the considered opinion that because cougars were not endangered in most of their range in America, there was no need to make them a priority species in Australia. Therefore, Malina would have to remain in the United States.

Their decision left me feeling very uncomfortable. All apex predators survive precariously. It is extraordinarily difficult to bring a predatory mammal species back after they land on the endangered list. I felt it was better to keep them off the list in the first place. Malina could have served as the "spokes-cat" for everything from Sumatran tigers to cheetahs. ARAZPA's profound lack of support would be a recurring theme as I continued to battle my way through the red tape of bureaucracy.

It was taking too long to get Malina to Australia, so I needed to get her more permanent housing in the States. Fortunately, I had fantastic friends at Wildlife Images near Grants Pass, Oregon. This wildlife rehabilitation facility was the best in the country, run by a family totally dedicated to helping wildlife. They agreed to take Malina and house her in a beautiful enclosure, complete with shady trees and grass under her feet. Steve came with me to Oregon, and we filmed her move to the new luxury accommodations.

Sadly, Malina never made it to Australia. About a year after her move to Wildlife Images, she got sick. She was taken to a vet and sedated for a complete examination. It turned out her kidneys were shutting down.

It could have been a genetic problem, or just old age. Either way, she never woke up.

One night, as I cooked dinner in our home on the zoo grounds, I brooded over my troubles. I didn't want to spend the evening feeling sorry for myself, so I thought about Steve out in the back, fire-gazing. He was a very lucky man, because for Steve, fire-gazing literally meant getting to build a roaring fire and sitting beside it, to contemplate life.

Suddenly I heard him come thundering up the front stairs. He burst wild-eyed into the kitchen. *He's been nailed by a snake,* I thought immediately. I didn't know what was going on.

"I know what we have to do!" he said, extremely excited.

He pulled me into the living room, sat me down, and took my hands in his. Looking intensely into my eyes, he said, "Babe, we've got to have children."

Wow, I thought, *that must have been some fire.*

"Ok-aaay," I said.

"You don't understand, you don't understand!" he said, trying to catch me up to his thoughts. "Everything we've been working for, the zoo that we've been building up, all of our efforts to protect wildlife, it will all stop with us!"

As with every good idea that came into his head, Steve wanted to act on it immediately. *Just take it in stride,* I said to myself. But he was so sincere. We'd talked about having children before, but for some reason it hit him that the time was now.

"We have *got* to have children," he said. "I know that if we have kids, they will carry on when we're gone."

"Great," I said. "Let's get right on that."

Steve kept pacing around the living room, talking about all the advantages of having kids—how I'd been so passionate about carrying on with the family business back in Oregon, and how he felt the same way about the zoo. He just knew our kids would feel the same too.

I said, "You know, there's no guarantee that we won't have a son who grows up to be a shoe salesman in Malaysia."

"Come off the grass," Steve said. "Any kid of ours is going to be a wildlife warrior."

I thought of the whale calves following

their mamas below the cliffs of the Great Australian Bight and prepared myself for a new adventure with Steve, maybe the greatest adventure of all.

CHAPTER TEN

Animal Planet

We were in far north Queensland, enjoying one of our many trips to Cape York Peninsula. We spent a lot of time with crocs in the wild here, and at the end of the trip, Steve had an idea. "I want to show you something," he said, inviting me along on a drive. Usually such an invitation led to some new experience in the bush, or an exciting encounter with wildlife. This one was an encounter with an animal, all right, but it wasn't in the bush.

Steve was uncharacteristically quiet and subdued as we drove, and when we arrived at our destination, I understood why.

A croc farm.

It was a great expanse of land. A single one of the enclosures on the farm could have held our whole zoo. The breeding ponds were immense—and overcrowded.

As soon as we arrived, Steve headed straight for the crocodile enclosures. Once inside, there were no fences or barriers to separate us from the big, territorial male crocs or the nesting females. There were only narrow, vehicle-wide tracks between the breeding ponds. The sense of exposure and vulnerability had me on edge. It was so different from the careful, respectful relationship we maintained with our own zoo crocs.

"What'll we do?" I asked Steve, eyeing the big salties on either side.

"See these clubs, babe?" he said, picking one up from a whole collection that lay alongside the track. "They use these to belt the crocs."

As we walked the narrow strip of land between the ponds, Steve and I dodged strikes from male salties more than sixteen feet long, and from the aggressive, nesting females. We could be ambushed virtually anytime from any direction. If one crocodile came too close to another, they would even attack each other.

We visited the farm's nursery, where the

eggs were hatched after collection and the babies were raised. I couldn't wrap my mind around it. Every hatchling there would be used for the skin and meat trade. I wasn't prepared for what I was about to see.

It was the equivalent of the most heinous POW camp you could imagine. Steve and I entered a large shed filled with rows of lidded boxes. Rock-and-roll music spilled full blast from speakers mounted on the ceiling. The room was completely dark. One of the workers switched on the lights and lifted up one of the lids.

Inside the box were a dozen or more small crocodiles, one or two feet long. So far, they had spent the whole of their existence inside such boxes. The baby crocs cowered pathetically as soon as the light hit their eyes.

The worker lashed out with his stick. He bashed the crocs to force them into the corners of the box, striking them repeatedly, hard, wherever the stick happened to land. It took all my will not to scream "Stop!" and rip the stick out of his hands. What did he think he was doing?

Steve looked at me, and I could tell he felt the same urge. "We're on their turf now, mate," he said to me quietly, meaning the croc farmers. As much as we wanted to right the evils of this cruel place, the business of crocodile farming was perfectly legal.

The little crocs had no fight left in them. As they cowered, beaten back, the worker tossed meat to them. Then he slammed shut the lid of the box, plunging the baby crocodiles into darkness once more. That is how farm-raised crocs exist for the first three years of their lives, in a crowded, pitch-black prison, with constant, blaring music—then a sudden blast of light, a beating, and some food.

When the babies graduated up to the subadult pond, they lived among an overcrowded, tangled mass of three-, four-, and five-foot crocodiles. In these stagnant, putrid ponds, Steve and I saw injuries suffered from fighting over food and space: severed limbs, parts of jaws torn off, and great chunks bitten out of their tails.

I felt as though I had entered a nightmare. The prevalence of birth defects horrified me: knots and stumpy burls where a tail was supposed to be, flippers instead of feet, crossed scissor-jaws. After half a dozen miserable years, the farm crocs would cop a bullet to their skulls when they grew large enough.

In another corner of the farm, the carcasses were processed. Their skins were sent out to adorn people for clothing, and their flesh was sold bush meat–style.

I'd seen Steve in countless situations that required great physical and emotional strength. He suffered the rigors of the bush without complaint. But seeing him in that croc farm that day made me realize he needed every ounce of his strength to witness the animals he loved so much treated in such a sadistic, inhumane manner. He had a lump in his throat that he just couldn't swallow.

How crocodile farming could be allowed in a country that was fighting to stop whaling and the bear bile trade was beyond me. I could not understand how anyone could proudly wear reptile-skin boots considering the torturous conditions under which the skins were obtained.

I left the farm that day shaken and confused.

"Why did you bring me there?" I asked. I knew the answer without Steve saying anything. He was doing me a favor. It's much easier to talk about something that you've actually seen and experienced.

"It's the farming that is evil," Steve said. "Not the people involved. Not all of them are wicked monsters, you know. Those blokes, I know them. They beat the crocodiles because they're afraid of them, or because that's what they were told to do."

Steve told me that a lot of crocodile behavior research, scientific studies, and filming was done at croc farms.

"It's an easy place to access crocodiles in great numbers," he said.

"But there's no way on earth you could ever observe any form of natural behavior there," I said.

Steve nodded grimly. While we were at the farm, we had witnessed females who were defending their nests being beaten back into submission, something that would never happen in the wild. The farm had some of the biggest crocs I'd ever seen. They were beautiful animals, living in squalor.

Croc farmers were fiercely protective of their livelihood and ignored efforts to control or regulate them or provide alternatives, such as ecotourism. A few of them arrogantly described themselves in public as "crocodile conservationists." I found this disgustingly deceptive. Killing crocs for money is not conservation.

As we started our long drive back to the zoo, we stopped at what could be called a general store. There was a pub attached to the establishment, and the store itself sold a wide variety of goods, groceries, cooking utensils, swags, clothing, shoes, even toys. As we picked up supplies in the shop, we passed the open doorway to the pub. A few of the patrons recognized Steve from television. We could hear them talking about him. The comments weren't exactly positive.

Steve didn't look happy. "Let's just get out of here," I whispered.

"Right-o," he said.

One of the pub patrons was louder than the others. "I'm a crocodile hunter too," he bragged. "Only I'm the real crocodile hunter. The real one, you hear me, mate?"

The braggart made his living at the stuffy trade, he informed his audience. A stuffy is a baby crocodile mounted by a taxidermist to be sold as a souvenir. To preserve their skins, hunters killed stuffys in much the same way that the bear poachers in Oregon stabbed their prey.

"We drive screwdrivers right through their eyes," Mister Stuffy boasted, eyeing Steve through the doorway of the pub. "Right through the bloody eye sockets!"

He was feeling his beer. We gathered up our purchases and headed out to the Ute. *Okay,* I said to myself, *we're going to make it. Just two or three more steps . . .*

Steve turned around and headed back toward the pub.

I'd never seen him like that before. My husband changed into somebody I didn't know. His eyes glared, his face flushed, and his lower lip trembled. I followed him to the threshold of the pub.

"Why don't you blokes come outside and tell me all about stuffys in the car park here?" he said. I couldn't see very well in the darkness of the pub interior, but I knew there were six or eight drinkers with Mister Stuffy.

I thought, *What is going to happen here?* There didn't seem any possible good outcomes. The pub drinkers stood up and filed out to face Steve. A half dozen against one.

Steve chose the biggest one, who Mister Stuffy seemed to be hiding behind.

"Bring it on, mate," Steve said. "Or are you only tough enough to take on baby crocs, you son of a bitch?"

Then Steve seemed to grow. I can't explain it. His fury made him tower over a guy who actually had a few inches of height on him and outweighed him with a whole beer gut's worth of weight. I couldn't imagine how he appeared to the pub drinkers, but he was scaring *me*.

They backed down. All six of them. Not one wanted to muck with Steve, who was clearly out of his mind with anger. All the world's croc farms, all the cruelty and ignorance that made animals suffer the world over, came to a head in the car park of the pub that evening.

Steve got into the truck. We drove off, and he didn't say anything for a long time.

"I don't understand," I finally said in the darkness of the front seat, as the bush landscape rolled by us. "What were they talking about? Were they killing crocs in the wild? Or were they croc farmers?"

I heard a small exhalation from Steve's side of the truck. I couldn't see his face in the gloom. I realized he was crying. I was astounded. This was the man I had just seen turn into a furious monster. Five minutes earlier I'd been convinced I was about to see him take on a half-dozen blokes bare-fisted. Now he wept in the darkness.

All at once, he sat up straight. With his jaw set, he wiped the tears from his face and composed himself. "I've known bastards like that all my life," he said. "Some people don't just *do* evil. Some people *are* evil."

He had told me before, but that night in the truck it hit home: Steve lived for wildlife and he would die for wildlife. He came by his convictions sincerely, from the bottom of his heart.

He was more than just my husband that night. He was my hero.

The word of the Crocodile Hunter spread, and we discovered that people overseas were starting to notice Steve as well. Peter Jennings, the respected anchor of ABC's *World News Tonight,* happened to see one of our documentaries. Every week Jennings featured a different individual as his "Person of the Week." Jennings chose to honor

Steve, featuring him in a long segment and naming him the person of the week.

I understood more than Steve what an honor this was, because as an American, I was more familiar with Peter Jennings. I knew firsthand the significance of this recognition. Steve was appreciative, but humble about it all. I felt the Jennings segment was a point of pride, simply because all of Steve's hard work was finally getting some recognition.

It took awhile, but that first glimmer of visibility eventually led to increased interest in our documentaries in America. The Discovery Channel, which was the gold standard of documentary cable television in the States, came calling.

Steve's and my partnership had evolved to the point where I was taking on more and more of the business side of the enterprise, both at the zoo and with our film work. My experience running a business at Westates Flagman proved invaluable. Steve didn't want to be cooped up with a calculator and balance sheets, but I actually enjoyed it. It was just another way that we completed each other.

I recall the first meeting I ever had with

the programming executives at the Discovery Channel. I arrived at their offices in Bethesda, Maryland, the sleek, modern headquarters of what was becoming one of the fastest-growing cable channels of the mid-1990s.

I was intimidated by the building, the big city, and the men in suits. I'm a real blue-jeans-and-T-shirt girl at heart. I had nothing to wear. I worried how I would handle myself in this oh-so-sophisticated environment. Finally I dug out one of my old power suits from the eighties, with padded shoulders and flared lapels.

My suit and I entered a room full of producers, attorneys, and several others—I wasn't even sure what they all did or why they were there. I didn't know what I was supposed to do. I kicked myself for not preparing a whole presentation. So I did the only thing I knew how to do. I talked about wildlife, our love for it, and our commitment to its conservation.

"I'm excited to have the opportunity to work with Discovery," I concluded. "Steve and I have always loved the channel. You do such quality shows. We want to be part of your family."

Hmm, we'll see about that. That was the response in the room as I read it. Then the lights went down, and we all stared at an enormous TV monitor to watch a Crocodile Hunter documentary. There I was, and there Steve was. I so much wanted everyone in the room to love him.

Well, our documentary ended, the lights came back up, and it was clear that the programmers at the Discovery Channel were a bit hesitant about Steve.

One of the executive producers was a woman named Maureen. "Terri, you see, there's a specific format for documentary filming," she said carefully. "The main focus is not on the host, but rather on the show's subject."

"The subject, yes," one of the other execs murmured.

Maureen was right. Up until that time, wildlife documentaries were made up of 80 percent wildlife, 20 percent host. What I had just shown her was a documentary where Steve was in almost every single shot.

"If you just put one of our shows on," I pleaded, "I know it will rate really well." I could hear myself. I knew I was echoing what countless filmmakers had said in that same room countless times before. The Discovery programmers had encountered filmmakers as naive as me a million times before. I didn't care. I knew I was right.

"It will work," I said.

Maureen gave me a patient smile. Everyone else in the room nodded thoughtfully. They all rose to their feet at once.

So, I figured, no go.

Then something interesting happened. Discovery had a subsidiary channel, just starting out, called Animal Planet—it wasn't too big or established, with a mere 250,000 subscribers. It had launched in 1996 and was still just a blip on the cultural radar. Nobody was quite sure whether it would last.

But Animal Planet had a different reaction to our show. The executives were eager to try something totally new.

"We want to air your documentaries, all of them, in the same form as you aired them in Australia," Animal Planet's executive vice president and general manager, Clark Bunting, told us, genuinely excited.

Sold. Just getting our shows on television in America was a big deal. But it was just the beginning.

CHAPTER ELEVEN

Bindi Sue

Dateline is a major prime-time news show in America, reaching millions of viewers on the NBC network. So it should have been very good news when the show's producers informed us that they wanted to do a segment on Steve, and they wanted to film it in Queensland.

"We want to experience him firsthand in the bush," the producer told me cheerfully over the phone.

Do you really, mate? I wanted to say. I had been with Steve in the bush. It was the most fantastic experience, but I wasn't sure he understood how remote the bush really was. I simply responded with all the right words about how excited we were to have *Dateline* come film.

The producers wanted two totally different environments in which to film. We chose the deserts of Queensland with the most venomous snake on earth, and the Cape York mangroves—crocodile territory. Great! responded *Dateline*. Perfect!

Only . . . the host was a woman, who had to look presentable, so she needed a generator for her blow-dryer. And a Winnebago, because it wasn't really fair to ask her to throw a swag on the ground among the scorpions and spiders. This film shoot would mean a bit of additional expense. We weren't just grabbing Sui and the Ute and setting out. But the exposure we would get on *Dateline* would be good for wildlife conservation, our zoo, and tourism.

I telephoned a representative of the Queensland Tourism and Travel Commission in Los Angeles. "I wonder if you could help us out," I asked. "This *Dateline* segment will showcase Queensland to people in America." Could Queensland Tourism possibly subsidize the cost of a generator and a Winnebago?

Silence at the end of the line. "What you are showing off of Queensland," a voice carefully explained, "is not how we want tourists to see our fair country." The most venomous snake on earth? Giant crocodiles? No, thanks.

"But people are fascinated by dangerous animals," I began to argue. I was wasting my time. There was no convincing him.

We scraped up the money ourselves, and off we went with the *Dateline* crew into the bush.

I saw our familiar stomping ground in Windorah through the eyes of our American visitors, who were as astounded as I had been at Steve's ability to bring the desert to life. We searched and searched for fierce snakes, but to no avail. Then Steve's sixth sense kicked in. At five thirty one morning, after days of fruitless searching, he said, "Hurry up, let's get going."

Our *Dateline* host was keen. This was what she'd traveled halfway around the world to see. "Where are we heading?" she asked.

"We've got to get out on the black soil plains," Steve said. "We are going to see a fierce snake at seven thirty."

The host looked a bit surprised. Even I teased him. "Oh, yeah, seven thirty, Stevo, we are going to see a fierce snake at *exactly* seven thirty, right."

But off we trundled to the black soil plains, camera crew, host, Winnebago, Ute—the whole convoy. Steve scanned the landscape. I monitored the temperature (and the clock). Seven thirty came and went.

"So, we're going to see a fierce snake at seven thirty?" I said. "Let's see, oh, yes, it *is* seven thirty, and where might the fierce snake be?"

After a little bit of teasing, Steve gave a good-natured grin, but then a look of determination passed over his face. No lie: Precisely at 7:32, he spotted a fierce snake. We ended up filming not one but two that morning.

The rest of the NBC crew looked upon Steve with new respect. This guy says we're going to see a snake at seven thirty and he's off by two minutes? They were checking their watches and shaking their heads.

Always give Steve the benefit of the doubt in the bush. I had learned that lesson before, the last time we had tailed fierce snakes on the black soil plains. But his ability to sense wildlife continued to strike me as uncanny.

We pulled up stakes and headed north to croc country. Lakefield National Park is one of my favorite places in Australia. Steve considered it the most beautiful place on the face of the earth. He gave the NBC people everything they wanted and more. Not only did we spot numerous saltwater crocodiles, but Steve found one that had submerged under an overhanging tree limb. We were able to crawl out on the limb and film straight down over a magnificent twelve-foot croc.

But it was left to me to head off what could have been a potential catastrophe at the end of filming. The *Dateline* host and a female producer were with a couple of the NBC crew members beside a stretch of water. Steve, myself, and some of the team from Australia Zoo faced them across the creek.

"See how NBC *Dateline* is over there on the other side?" Steve said. "Let's show them *our* NBC 'Datelines,' what do you reckon?"

All the guys laughed. They turned around, faced their backsides toward our

American friends, and were about to drop their daks. I leaped forward like a soldier throwing herself over a grenade.

"Noooooo!" I exclaimed. "The women from New York just won't get it."

The boys grumpily kept their pants on. Steve threw me an oh-you're-no-fun look. I may have been a wet blanket, but a cross-cultural disaster had been successfully averted.

Our life together was filled with contrasts. One week we were croc hunting with *Dateline* in Cape York. Only a short time after that, Steve and I found ourselves out of our element entirely, at the CableACE Award banquet in Los Angeles.

Steve was up for an award as host of the documentary *Ten Deadliest Snakes in the World*. He lost out to the legendary Walter Cronkite. Any time you lose to Walter Cronkite, you can't complain too much. After the awards ceremony, we got roped into an after-party that was not our cup of tea.

Everyone wore tuxedos. Steve wore khaki. Everyone drank, smoked, and made small talk, none of which Steve did at all. We got separated, and I saw him across the room looking quite claustrophobic. I sidled over.

"Why don't we just go back up to our room?" I whispered into his ear. This proved to be a terrific idea. It fit in nicely with our plans for starting a family, and it was quite possibly the best seven minutes of my life!

After our stay in Los Angeles, Steve flew directly back to the zoo, while I went home by way of one my favorite places in the world, Fiji. We were very interested in working there with crested iguanas, a species under threat. I did some filming for the local TV station and checked out a population of the brilliantly patterned lizards on the Fijian island of Yadua Taba.

When I got back to Queensland, I discovered that I was, in fact, expecting. Steve and I were over the moon. I couldn't believe how thrilled he was. Then, mid-celebration, he suddenly pulled up short. He eyed me sideways.

"Wait a minute," he said. "You were just in Fiji for two weeks."

"Remember the CableACE Awards? Where you got bored in that room full of tuxedos?"

He gave me a sly grin. "Ah, yes," he said,

satisfied with his paternity (as if there was ever any doubt!). We had ourselves an L.A. baby.

I visited the doctor. "This is a first for me," I said. "What do I do?"

"Just keep doing what you would normally do," the doctor said. "It's probably not a good time to take up skydiving, but it would be fine to carry on with your usual activities." I was thrilled to get Dr. Michael's advice. He had been the Irwin family doctor for years, and he definitely understood what our lifestyle entailed. I embarked on an ambitious schedule of filmmaking.

We named the life growing inside me "Igor." Steve and I were both sure we were having a boy. Both my sisters had boys, and somehow, Igor just seemed to fit. With Igor on board, it was ironic that our first documentary journey, to Tasmania, involved a family tragedy of epic proportions. Tasmania, the island off the southern coast of Australia, has unique wildlife and spectacular, temperate-zone rain forests. But as soon as we arrived, Steve and I were swept up in a whale beaching that was emotionally harrowing.

In a remote area on the western side of

the island, near the town of Marrawah, a pod of sperm whales was stranded on the beach. One big male came to shore first. Over the next twenty-four hours, another thirty-four whales stranded themselves, including calves and pregnant mothers.

Whale stranding is one of the heartbreaking mysteries of the animal world. It is little understood. At this moment no scientific reasoning mattered as we encountered the tragedy unfolding on that Tasmanian beach.

I felt so helpless. All I could do was be there as the huge, gorgeous sea mammals fought pitifully to stay alive. The weather was cold, even though it was officially the Tasmanian summer, and the seas were too rough to get a boat out to help the whales. We put our arms around the dying animals, spoke to them, and looked into their eyes to share in their pain and grief. By the end of the day I was so cold that I had trouble getting my pants off over my pregnant belly. It took me half an hour of struggling in the car park to strip off my soaking-wet clothes and get into some warm, dry gear. Physically, emotionally, and even spiritually, it had been an exhausting day.

I pondered what communication the

baby inside me would have gotten from the event. The dying whales had sung among themselves. Steve and I spoke back and forth over their stranded bodies. What did baby Igor pick up on? Through our experiences, we were beginning to form our very own tiny wildlife warrior, even before the baby was born. Igor had only just begun his education. We left the beach to track Tasmanian snakes inland. Steve was feeling particularly protective of me.

"Whatever you do, don't grab any of these snakes," he said. "They are all venomous here in Tasmania. You are pregnant and you've got to be careful."

"No problem," I said. But it did turn out to be difficult just to watch. Over and over again, Steve got to wrangle a gorgeous venomous snake as the crew filmed. I wanted some of the action!

After a few days of this, we tramped through the bush and encountered a great big tiger snake. It glistened in the sun at the edge of a stream. Steve turned around and motioned to the cameraman to start rolling. We made minimal movements and whispered, even though snakes have no ears and can't hear (instead they sense vibrations).

We approached the tiger snake as it drank in the stream. It raised its head slightly. It knew we were there. My heart started pounding, but I had made a decision. I knew we had one take with this snake. Once we disturbed it, it would never go back to drinking, and the shot would be lost.

I moved forward, waddling my pregnant body in behind the snake, and tailed him. He was a huge snake, but slow and gentle, just as I had anticipated. I told the camera all about tigers, how they could give birth to thirty young at once, and how the Tasmanian tiger snakes are special, tolerating some of the coldest weather in the country.

As I let the snake go, I looked sheepishly back at Steve. His eyes had grown large, and he didn't say a word. I'm not entirely sure if he was angry with me. I think he realized that I was still the same old Terri, even though I was pregnant.

Maybe it was my condition, but I was even more sensitive about cruelty to wildlife. When we journeyed to New Zealand to protest whale hunts, we viewed a documentary about whales attacking the whaling ships, trying to defend the females and their young. Whales are like elephants of the sea. They have family structures, mannerisms, and habits that are similar to our own.

In the midst of this very emotional work in Wellington, I felt the baby move for the first time. Soon the baby was dancing around inside me both day and night. All my check-ups came back favorable, and the doctor said Steve was more than welcome to glove up and help deliver the baby when the time came.

Until then, though, there was stacks of filming to be done. We filmed sharks just off the Queensland coast, near where Steve's parents had retired. Some of the crew were typical Aussie blokes. As soon as I got on board and they saw that I was very obviously pregnant, they decided to embark on "Project Spew." To attract sharks, they mixed up a large container of chum—a gory stew made of fish oil, blood, fish skeletons, and offal. The crew would pass it right underneath my nose in an effort to make me sick. I countered them by sitting down and eating lunch right next to the putrid-smelling churn container. I knew they couldn't break me!

We then headed for the Galapagos Islands, my last international trip before giving birth. Once I got back I would be too pregnant to fly. I would be grounded until the baby came.

We had to travel through Ecuador to get to the Galapagos Islands, and we stopped overnight in Quito on the way. It was a real culture shock to check in and discover that the doorman was packing a .357. Although I always felt safe with Steve, we had to be particularly careful where we filmed. At one point, shooting near a river, Steve turned to me and said, "Run for the van. Don't walk—run. And don't look back."

I waddled as fast as my fat little legs would carry me. When I'd reached the safety of the van, I took a chance and looked back. I could see a semicircle of local men closing in on the cameraman and crew. It occurred to me that our camera could probably buy the entire village. It was obviously a mistake to flash around so much expensive gear. Steve managed to get everyone into the van, and we sped off in the nick of time.

When we finally reached the Galapagos Islands, we stayed on the water in a catamaran. I was completely unprepared for the heat. Even on the boat there wasn't a breeze. The entire crew slept above deck. They were the smart ones. I was so hot that somehow Steve and John managed to negotiate for some ice. They'd take turns filling a washcloth with ice to cool down my giant tummy. There was an entire day when the baby didn't move, and I was worried. But everything was fine the next day, and I think Igor had just spread out like the rest of us, trying to keep cool.

The last filming I did while pregnant with baby Igor was off the Australian coast again, for a documentary on sharks. I was almost to the point where I couldn't go out on the boat anymore. I was so pregnant, I felt incredibly uncomfortable on the rolling seas. The constant bouncing of the boat was literally stretching my cervix. I went out for one last trip and spent most of my time lying on my side, holding my enormous belly.

Steve knew the sharks intimately by now. "The big tiger sharks will show up at eleven o'clock," he said. And sure enough, they did, right on the dot. We had the shark cage and the dinghy, with myself (and Igor), Steve, and Sui.

I sat in the dingy and watched the enormous tigers as they circled around. They had to be more than fourteen feet long, and some of them were larger than the boat itself. I quickly figured out that because of my great belly I was very unbalanced. I had to be careful so as not to tip the boat. Sui was an old hand at all of this. She planted herself in the center of the boat and lay down, sticking to the safest spot possible.

Steve enjoyed going into the cage. The sharks came up to him one by one, trying to open this strange container and get to the nice yummy food inside.

"They have a childlike curiosity," he told me, breaking to the surface before lowering himself down again. "They're really trying to figure out how to get me!"

I got to experience them on the surface, in the dinghy. Tiger sharks don't just feed under the water. They readily take food off the surface, too, and even lift themselves partially out of the water. Huge tiger sharks, wider across than I was (which at that point was saying a lot) came up to taste the boat, taste the motor, and put their heads all the way over the back of the dinghy.

I was fascinated and had to stop myself from reaching out and stroking them. Of course I didn't dare move, because I needed to counterbalance the boat, so the sharks wouldn't rock it over. After a day of filming, my opinion of sharks was even better. Steve was right. Bringing people into close proximity to wildlife was all you had to do. I fell in love with tiger sharks that day. As it turned out, that was the last documentary of my pregnancy. For the next few weeks I'd be restricted to working at the zoo.

Steve, on the other hand, had time to squeeze in one more doco. He and John headed to Indonesia to film Komodo dragons. Steve found one dragon with a fishhook in its mouth. The line was trailing alongside the eight-foot lizard, and Steve decided to help. He got in front of the huge predator and pulled until the hook popped free. It was at that moment that the dragon clicked. He homed in on Steve, raised his head, and gave chase. The Komodo was serious. Steve managed to scramble up a small tree, with the dragon at his feet. Luckily, it was just too big to climb well and only grabbed Steve on the boot.

Steve turned to the camera. "Danger, danger, danger!" was all he could get out. The Komodo dragon carries about sixteen types of bacteria in the long strings of drool that hang from its mouth. All it needs to do is break the skin, and its prey will die of infection. Although the dragon's tooth had sliced all the way through Steve's boot, it didn't penetrate his sock or his foot. "I'd rather take a hit from an eight-foot saltie than an eight-foot dragon," Steve said later.

When Steve made it home safe and sound, I encouraged my tummy, "Hurry up and be born, Igor, so we can hit the road again."

One evening Steve and I didn't feel like cooking, and we had ordered a pizza. I noticed that I was a bit leaky, but when you are enormously pregnant, all kinds of weird things happen with your body. I didn't pay any particular attention. The next day I called the hospital.

"You should come right in," the nurse told me over the phone. Steve was fairly nearby, on the Gold Coast south of Brisbane, filming bull sharks.

I won't bother him, I thought. I'll just go in for a quick checkup.

"If everything checks out okay," I told them at the hospital, "I'll just head back."

The nurse looked to see if I was serious. She laughed. "You're not going anywhere," she said. "You're having a baby."

I called Steve. He came up from the Gold Coast as quickly as he could, after losing his car keys, not remembering where he parked, and forgetting which way home was in his excitement.

When he arrived at the hospital, I saw that he had brought the whole camera crew with him. John was just as flustered as anyone but suggested we film the event.

"It's okay with me," Steve said. I was in no mood to argue. I didn't care if a spaceship landed on the hospital. Each contraction took every bit of my attention.

When they finally wheeled me into the delivery room at about eight o'clock that night, I was so tired I didn't know how I could go on. Steve proved to be a great coach. He encouraged me as though it were a footy game.

"You can do it, babe," he yelled. "Come on, push!"

At 9:46 p.m., a little head appeared. Steve was beside himself with excitement. I was in a fog, but I clearly remember the joy on his face. He helped turn and lift the baby out. I heard both Steve and doctor announce simultaneously, "It's a girl."

Six pounds and two ounces of little baby girl. She was early but she was fine. All pink and perfect.

Steve cut the umbilical cord and cradled her, gazing down at his newborn daughter. "Look, she's our little Bindi."

She was named after a crocodile at the zoo, and it also fit that the word "bindi" was Aboriginal for "young girl." Here was our own young girl, our little Bindi.

I smiled up at Steve. "Bindi Sue," I said, after his beloved dog, Sui.

Steve gently handed her to me. We both looked down at her in utter amazement. He suddenly scooped her up in the towels and blankets and bolted off.

"I've got a baby girl!" he yelled, as he headed down the hall. The doctor and midwives were still attending to me. After a while, one of the midwives said nervously, "So, is he coming back?"

I just laughed. I knew what Steve was doing. He was showing off his beautiful baby girl to the whole maternity ward, even though each and every new parent had their own bundle of joy. Steve was such a proud parent.

He came back and laid Bindi beside me. I said, "I couldn't have done it if you hadn't been here."

"Yes, you could have."

"No, I really needed you here."

Once again, I had that overwhelming feeling that as long as we were together, everything would be safe and wonderful. I watched Bindi as she stared intently at her daddy with dark, piercing eyes. He gazed back at her and smiled, tears rolling down his cheeks, with such great love for his new daughter. The world had a brand-new wildlife warrior.

CHAPTER TWELVE

The Crocodile Kid

Stephen Robert Irwin was born in Upper Ferntree Gully, outside of Melbourne, in 1962, on his mother's birthday, February 22.

Lynette and Robert Irwin—the people I always knew more familiarly as Lyn and Bob—exposed him to wildlife at an early age. Steve always described his household growing up as harboring a "menagerie." That meant an ever-expanding collection of tanks, terrariums, and cages with an ever-growing population of snakes and lizards.

Bob made an excellent living for his family as a plumber, but his true love was reptiles. Lyn was a maternity nurse, and she had a natural love of nurturing. She didn't limit herself to reptiles. She took in injured animals of all kinds.

On his sixth birthday, Steve received a scrub python as a gift from his parents. "Fred the scrubby was my best friend growing up," Steve said. "The problem was, he was so big, and I was still little. He could have eaten me without a worry."

Lyn and Bob moved their family north from the Melbourne area to Queensland in 1970. They purchased the original four-acre zoo property in Beerwah after a snake-finding trip. Eight-year-old Steve and his sisters, Joy and Mandy, helped install the family menagerie in what was at first called the Beerwah Reptile Park. The beautifully landscaped zoo grounds that I first encountered more than two decades later had originally started out as a cattle paddock.

Joy was the older sister, Mandy the younger, and Steve was in the middle. There were periods when the family lived in a caravan parked on the reptile park's grounds. Steve got along well with his sisters, and the usual sibling rivalry expressed itself in who could better care for the menagerie of animals taken in by the family. The study of wildlife was a household passion. Bob loved all reptiles, even venomous snakes. Lyn took in the injured and orphaned. They made a great team, and Steve was born directly from their example and teaching.

"Whenever we were driving," Steve told me, "if we saw a kangaroo on the side of the roadway that had been killed by a car, we always stopped." Mother and son would investigate the dead roo and, if it was female, check its pouch. They rescued dozens, maybe hundreds, of live kangaroo joeys this way, brought them home, and raised them.

"We had snakes and goannas mostly, but also orphaned roo joeys, sugar gliders, and possums," Steve said about these humble beginnings. "We didn't have enclosures for crocodiles. That came later, after my parents became sick to death of the hatred they saw directed toward crocs."

I soon became aware that as much as Steve loved his parents equally, he got different things from each of them. Bob was his hero, his mentor, the man he wanted to become. Bob's knowledge of reptile—and especially snake—behavior made him an invaluable resource for academics all over the country. The Queensland Museum wanted to investigate the ways of the secretive fierce snake, and Bob shared their passion. When the administrators of the Queensland

Parks and Wildlife Service wanted to relocate problem crocodilians, they called Bob.

Meanwhile, Lyn became, in Steve's words, "the Mother Teresa of animal rescue." Lyn designed a substitute pouch for orphaned roo and wallaby joeys. She came up with appropriate formulas to feed them too. Lyn created the warm, nurturing environment that made Steve's dreams, goals, and aspirations real and reachable. Steve was always a boy who loved his mum, and Lyn was the matriarch of the family. While Bob and Steve were fearless around taipans and saltwater crocs, they had the utmost respect for Lyn. She was a pioneering wildlife rehabilitator who set the mark for both Steve and myself.

From the very first, I was welcomed into the Irwin family. The greatest thing was that I felt Lyn and Bob loved me not just because I was married to Steve, but for myself, for who I was. That gave me confidence to feel at home as a new arrival to Australia.

"He was a little monster," Bob said, laughing, about Steve as a child. The main difficulty wasn't unruly behavior. It was Steve's insatiable curiosity about the bush and the wildlife in it.

"For the first few months, when he was a baby, I could put Steve down and he would stay where I put him," Lyn told me. "But after he started to get around on his own, it was all over. I would find him either on the roof or up in some tree."

When the family headed off on a trip, usually to North Queensland on wildlife jaunts, Steve could always be counted on to be elsewhere when they were ready to go. They would find him next to the nearest stream, snagging yabbies or turning over bits of wood to see what was hidden underneath.

"He was never where we wanted him to be," Lyn recalled with a laugh.

Steve's childhood was "family, wildlife, and sport," he told me. He played rugby league for the Caloundra Sharks in high school and was picked to play rugby for the Queensland Schoolboys and represent the state, but he chose to go on a field trip with his dad to catch reptiles instead.

Sometimes sport and wildlife mixed in unexpected ways. Bob was an expert badminton player, and a preteen Steve decided to lay out a badminton court in the family's backyard one day. He had a brolga as a friend, a large bird that he called Brolly. Brolly objected to Steve rearranging her territory. She waited until his back was turned and then attacked. *Wham!* A brolga's beak is a fearsome weapon, and Brolly's slammed into the back of little Stevo's head.

His bird friend knocked him out cold.

"Go ahead, feel it," Steve said after regaling me with this story. He bent his head. I could still feel a knot of scar tissue, a souvenir of the brolga attack years earlier.

During a cricket match one afternoon, Steve was called up to bat on the second drop, but he was out for a duck. He became bored during the subsequent stretch of inactivity and investigated a nearby creek. Beneath an abandoned sheet of corrugated iron, Steve encountered a red-bellied black snake. Red-bellies are venomous. Steve knew this, but he thought that his father would prize a red-bellied black snake to add to the family's menagerie. So a very young Steve tailed the red-belly.

Steve instinctively dodged each of the snake's strikes, but he was now stuck for something to put the snake in, and it was becoming more aggressive by the second. "Finally one of me mates brought over our bus driver's esky," he said. "I dumped out all his sandwiches and managed to get him in. He was one cranky snake!"

To the cheers and wonderment of his cricket teammates, Steve caught another half-dozen red-bellies that afternoon. The bus driver didn't realize that there were snakes on the bus, but when he found out, he made a point of telling Steve's dad.

Bob was less than pleased. Steve, expecting to be praised, got a harsh reprimand instead. "Dad sunk a boot up my bum," was how Steve explained the aftermath of the snakes-in-the-esky incident. Bob railed against Steve's thoughtlessness for endangering his mates and the bus driver by bringing live venomous snakes into their midst.

Lyn's passion for rehabilitation and Bob's passion for crocodiles meshed together to prompt a new effort to save "problem" crocodiles by relocating them to areas where they would not bother humans.

Bob pioneered a kinder, gentler way to do it. At that point in time, the accepted method of croc capture was a cruel one. Park rangers and animal control officers would sink a barbed harpoon into the animal's hide. They would then reel in the thrashing, bleeding croc. Oftentimes the harpoons would go astray and miss their mark, or the barbs would tear themselves out during the struggle, leaving a gaping, jagged hole.

"The way they were doing it," Steve said, "there was maybe a one-in-five chance of success."

His father's approach was quite different, and quite ingenious, involving such practices as jumping, soft mesh trapping, and netting. The approach grew out of Bob's knowledge of crocodilian behavior. Crocs are ambush predators, snatching their prey by lunging onto land from the water. Bob lured them to a trap with fresh meat, usually a feral pig. He hung a fist-sized piece of meat as lead-in bait in front of a trawler-mesh trap.

Saltwater crocs are very intelligent and wary of traps. The "free" feed would give them a sense of security, and they wouldn't worry about the new thing in their territory. Then, after the lead-in bait disappeared a

Steve's mother always said,
"If I couldn't see him, he was either on the roof or up in some tree."

A young Irwin family:
Steve, Joy, Lyn, Bob, and Mandy.

A young Steve. He jumped his
first croc at only nine years old.

In the early days, Steve did all his crocodile work in the bush, on his own.

Steve and me, when we first met.

Walking Malina, my rescued cougar,
on the beach in Oregon.

Malina and me, when I ran Cougar Country.

Our wedding day, June 4, 1992.
From left to right: Julia Raines, Bob Irwin, me, Steve, Lyn Irwin, and Clarence Raines.

Mates for life: Wes and Steve.

Steve was always hands-on with the construction work at the zoo.

Soul mates.

Steve and his “girlfriend,” Sui.

Meeting a Bennetts wallaby while filming in Tasmania.

Family, wildlife, and surfing—Steve's three great loves.

"If I could be remembered for any one thing," Steve said, "I'd like to be remembered as a good dad."

Rocky Mountain National Park, Colorado.

Steve in Antarctica . . . Where's your coat?

Together in Texas, filming for the Travel Channel.

At 175 years old,
Harriet was our oldest and dearest friend.

Steve's greatest inspiration—his mother, Lyn.

The whole family, in the bush,
aboard Steve's research vessel, *Croc One*.

Our last trip together, doing crocodile research in Cape York Peninsula, Queensland, Australia.

few nights in a row, Bob placed fresh meat deep within the trap.

The target crocodile would enter, pull on the meat (which released a trigger mechanism), and trip a weight bag. When the weight bag fell, it pulled the mouth of the trap shut like a drawstring, preventing the crocodile from escaping. Then came the tricky part. Bob and young Steve had to pin the croc by laying themselves on top of it. Bob would peel back the mesh, blindfold the animal and duct-tape its jaws, and then transport it in the trap or in a croc box.

The process developed by trial and error over the course of many years. Steve would later perfect it. There was no doubt that it was vastly superior to a harpoon barb. There is nothing, of course, more invasive than a bullet, and the crocs Bob captured faced a stark choice: They would be shot by their angry, fearful human neighbors, or relocated to safer environments. Bob preferred the momentary discomfort of the captured croc to seeing it lying dead on a riverbank.

Bob brought his young son along on his crocodilian relocation work. "I got so I could work the spotty, and Dad would jump the smaller ones," Steve said. "He tossed them into the bottom of the boat, and I would dive on top to pin them. They used to thrash me, putting up a good fight." Steve didn't officially perform his first capture until he was nine years old. Father and son had been working together on croc relocation for a couple of years by then.

The Queensland Parks and Wildlife Service was confident that Bob's croc-catching expertise could help remove a group of freshies on the Leichhardt River. Freshwater crocs are smaller, with long, narrow jaws. They are less aggressive than the saltwater variety, but they still have fearsome sets of teeth and can lash out when cornered.

Steve and Bob worked together for several nights, moving one freshie after another out of a section of river that was about to be dammed. On their last night, while Bob wrangled one croc in the boat, Steve caught the red-eye shine of another with his spotlight.

He alerted his father. "Get up in front," Bob said. "Hold him with your spotty."

That's when Steve realized that this capture was going to be different. He was in the front of the boat—which meant that he would be the one leaping on top of the croc in the water.

"Bob and I both thought it was a small one," Steve recalled.

"But it wasn't," I said.

"It was bigger than I was," Steve said, shaking his head in disbelief at the memory.

Bob made him wait until the last possible moment to jump. Steve kept his light shining into the croc's eyes.

"Okay, I got him," Bob said. He turned his own torch on and shined the croc. That was Steve's signal to drop his own spotty and get ready to jump.

"Wait, wait, wait," Bob cautioned, and the dinghy moved closer. Bob could barely contain his son, who was bursting with excitement. "Now!"

Steve leaped. As soon as he did, he realized that he had misjudged the croc's size. It wasn't a three-footer. It was more like four or five feet long, easily matching his weight.

The croc dove. *No matter what, I'm not letting go,* Steve thought. There was no way he was going to let his dad down. Just as Steve was about to run out of air, he felt his father's strong arm reach down to bring both Steve and the croc into the boat.

Steve told me that when he looked at Bob's face, he could see both worry and pride. Worry because Steve had actually been out of sight in the murky water for a long moment—and pride because he made a perfect capture, his first time out.

"Dad started grinning from ear to ear," Steve recalled. "I had jumped my first croc. Even though I was only nine, it was one of the biggest moments of my life."

Bob and Lyn set Steve on the path he traveled in life. What was incredible about Steve was how much he made it his own. He took the example of his parents and ran with it.

In 1980 Bob and Lyn decided to change the Beerwah Reptile Park to the Queensland Reptile and Fauna Park, the name under which I would first encounter it. Angry at the senseless slaughter of crocodilians, Bob began to expand the zoo to create habitats for rescued crocs.

I can pinpoint the exact period when Steve grew into the man who would become so well known to people around the world as the Crocodile Hunter. It was the time he spent alone, with his first dog, Chilli, in the bush for months at a time, trapping and relocating crocs for the government.

At the start of the 1980s, Steve was eighteen, a recent graduate of Caloundra State High School, and still under his father's tutelage. Ten years later he had been transformed. He proved himself capable of doing some of the most dangerous wildlife work in the world, solo and with spectacular results. Years in the wilderness lent him a deep understanding of the natural world. More than that, he had reinforced a unique connection with wildlife that would stay with him throughout his whole life.

The legend of a giant black saltie in Cape York had been growing for years. It haunted a river system in north Queensland and eluded all attempts at capture or death. In 1988 the East Coast Crocodile Management Program enlisted Bob and Steve to remove this "problem" crocodile and relocate him back to their zoo.

It was a difficult assignment. At first they could find no sign of the mythical black croc. Perhaps it was a figment of the public imagination, tying together several incidents and sightings to create a single animal out of many. For months, Bob and Steve surveyed the mangrove swamps and riverbanks, finally locating a telltale belly slide that betrayed the presence of a huge male.

Then Bob gave his son the ultimate vote of confidence. He left him alone.

Bob went back to Beerwah. It was just Steve and his dog, Chilli. The huge saltwater crocodile had repeatedly outwitted hunters with high-powered rifles and "professionals" from crocodile farms sent in to exterminate him. Steve took up a hunt that had already lasted for years. Only he planned to save this modern-day dinosaur rather than kill it.

One night the croc almost took him instead. He spotted a smaller female and set a net across the river to snare her. But something was wrong. An incredible force pulled the net upstream, against the current and against all logic. Steve started his outboard, but it didn't help. The bow of his boat pitched downward, taking on water. He rushed to cut the net free before the croc swamped the boat.

He needn't have bothered. The bow of the boat suddenly surged upward and the net hung limp. Steve pulled it in and found a gaping hole as big as his dinghy. The heavy-duty trawler mesh had been torn straight through.

Another evening, Steve and Chilli watched a half-dozen feral pigs swim across the river. As the animals clambered up the opposite bank, the hindmost pig seemed to slip suddenly back into the water and disappear, without a thrash or squeal. Steve didn't even see the big croc. It had been a stealth attack.

Stalking the black ghost, Steve became one with the river. He spent months at a time in the bush. He disregarded the mangrove mud that covered him until he was camouflaged as he sat silently in wait. He learned the river systems of the area like the back of his hand.

Then the croc made his move. Steve discovered that the lead-in bait for one of his traps had been eaten, grabbed down with such force that its nylon cord had wound up high in a mangrove tree. Steve chose a particularly smelly chunk of meat to bait the trap the next night. He placed it downstream and made his way through the swamp on foot, so he would leave no sign of his approach on the riverbank.

The next two days, nothing. Steve re-baited the trap, this time using the carcass of a whole boar. He woke in the middle of the night. Chilli had alerted him that something had disturbed the peace of the mangroves. Steve would have to wait until daylight to check the trap.

The next morning, Steve took his boat out and saw what had happened. The big male had triggered the trap and was snared in the mesh—sort of. Even though the rectangular-shaped net was the biggest he had, the croc's tail and back leg stuck out. But the black ghost had finally been caught.

At Steve's approach, the animal thrashed wildly, smashing apart mangrove trees on either side of the trap. Steve tried to top-jaw-rope the croc, but it was fighting too violently. Normally Chilli acted as a distraction, giving Steve the chance to secure the croc. But the dog wanted no part of this. She cowered on the floor of the dinghy, unwilling to face this monstrously large croc. Steve was truly on his own.

He finally secured a top-jaw rope and tied the other end to a tree. With a massive "death roll"—a defensive maneuver in which the reptile spins its enormous body—

the big croc smashed the tree flat and snapped it off. Steve tried again; the croc thrashed, growling and roaring in protest at the trapper in khaki, lunging again and again to tear Steve apart.

Finally, the giant croc death-rolled so violently that he came off the bank and landed in the boat, which immediately sank. Chilli had jumped out and was swimming for shore as Steve worked against time. With the croc underwater, Steve lashed the croc, trap and all, in the dinghy. But moving the waterlogged boat and a ton of crocodile was simply too much. Steve sprinted several miles in the tropical heat to reach a cane farm, where he hoped to get help. The cane farmers were a bit hesitant to lend a hand, so Steve promised them a case of beer, and a deal was made. With a sturdy fishing boat secured to each side of Steve's dinghy, they managed to tow it downriver where they could winch croc and boat onto dry land to get him into a crate. By this time, a crowd of spectators had gathered.

When Steve told me the story of the capture, I got the sense that he felt sorry he had to catch the crocodile at all.

"It seemed wrong to remove the king of

the river," Steve said. "That croc had lasted in his territory for decades. Here I was taking him out of it. The local people just seemed relieved, and a couple even joked about how many boots he'd make."

Steve was very clever to include the local people and soon won them over to see just how special this crocodile really was. Just as he was dragged into his crate, the old croc attempted a final act of defiance, a death roll that forced Steve to pin him again.

"I whispered to him to calm him down," Steve said.

"What did you say to him?" I asked.

"'Please don't die.'"

The black crocodile didn't die. Steve brought him back to Beerwah, named him Acco, and gave him a beautiful big pond that Bob had prepared, with plenty of places to hide.

We were in the Crocodile Environmental Park at the zoo when Steve first told me the story of Acco's capture. I just had to revisit him after hearing his story. There he was, the black ghost himself, magnificently sunning on the bank of his billabong.

Standing there next to this impressive animal, I tried to wrap my mind around the idea that people had wanted him dead. His huge, intimidating teeth made him look primeval, and his osteodermal plates gleamed black in the sun—a dinosaur, living here among us. I felt so emotional, contemplating the fear-based cruelty that prompted humans to hate these animals.

For his part, Acco still remembered his capture, even though it had happened nearly a decade before. Whenever Steve went into his enclosure, Acco would stalk him and strike, exploding out of the water with the intent to catch Steve unaware.

Despite the conflict in Steve's soul over whether he had done the right thing, I decided that Acco's capture had to be. In the zoo, Acco had his own territory to patrol and a beautiful female crocodile, Connie, who loved him dearly. Left in the wild, somebody would have eventually shot him. If the choice is between a bullet and living in the Crocodile Environmental Park, I think his new territory was much more preferable.

When I met Steve in 1991, he had just emerged from a solid decade in the bush, either with Bob or on his own, with just his dog Chilli, and later Sui. Those years had been like a test of fire. As a boy all Steve wanted to do was to be like his dad. At twenty-nine he'd become like Bob and then some.

He had done so much more than catch crocs. In the western deserts, he and Bob helped researchers from the Queensland Museum understand the intricacies of fierce snake behavior. Steve also embarked on a behavioral study of a rare and little-understood type of arboreal lizard, the canopy goanna, scrambling up into trees in the rain forests of Cape York Peninsula in pursuit of herpetological knowledge.

As much as Steve had become a natural for television, over the course of the 1980s he had become a serious naturalist as well. His hands-on experience, gleaned from years in the bush, meshed well with the more abstract knowledge of the academics. No one had ever accomplished what he had, tracking and trapping crocodiles for months at a time on his own.

He would hand on to Bindi and Robert his knowledge of nature and the bush, just as Bob and Lyn had handed it down to him. This is what few people understood about Steve—his relationship with his family, and the tradition of passion and commitment and understanding that passed from generation to generation.

Later on, that Irwin family tradition would bring Steve untold grief, when outsiders misjudged his effort to educate his children and crucified him for it.

CHAPTER THIRTEEN

On the Road Again

When Steve and I brought Bindi home in July of 1998, we felt complete. Now we were a family, and this beautiful baby girl would add a whole new dimension to our adventures. Sui, for her part, was less than thrilled with the new addition to the household, a little crying person the size of a loaf of bread. Sui's initial reaction reminded me of the reception I got from her when I first arrived.

"Listen, Sui," Steve said, talking to her intently as if she were human. "You need to take care of my little Bindi. You need to help me protect her."

From the expression on her face, it looked like she was thinking, *All right, I'll do it as a favor for you, Stevo, but I'm not that wild about it.*

The dead of winter on the Sunshine Coast is not exactly Antarctica. There is never any snow. But the old Queenslander we lived in on the zoo grounds was drafty and hard to heat, with high ceilings. It also had a lot of steps leading up to the front and back doors. The combination of stairs and a new baby made me nervous. Even keeping Bindi warm was challenging, but we made do. We brought in space heaters and bundled her up constantly. It made me realize that the cozy little brick house that Bob first built for his family really was a much better design.

We had been looking at some land adjoining the zoo and decided to purchase it in order to expand. There was a small house on the new property, nothing too grand, just a modest home built of brick, with three bedrooms and one bathroom. We liked the seclusion of the place most of all. The builder had tucked it in behind a macadamia orchard, but it was still right next door to the zoo. We could be part of the zoo yet apart from it at the same time. Perfect.

"Make this house exactly the way you

want it," Steve told me. "This is going to be our home."

He dedicated himself to getting us moved in. I knew this would be our last stop. We wouldn't be moving again. We laid new carpet and linoleum and installed reverse-cycle air-conditioning and heat. Ah, the luxury of having a climate-controlled house. I installed stained-glass windows in the bathroom with wildlife-themed panes, featuring a jabiru, a crocodile, and a big goanna. We also used wildlife tiles throughout, of dingoes, whales, and kangaroos. We made the house our own.

We worked on the exterior grounds as well. Steve transplanted palm trees from his parents' place on the Queensland coast and erected fences for privacy. He designed a circular driveway. As he laid the concrete, he put his own footprints and handprints in the wet cement. Then he ran into the house to fetch Bindi and me.

"Come on," he said. "Let's all do it." We grabbed Sui, too, and put her paw prints in, and then did Bindi, who was just eight months old. It took a couple of tries, but we got her handprints and her footprints as well, and then my own. We stood back and admired the time capsule we had created.

That afternoon the rains came. The Sunshine Coast is usually bright and dry, but when it rains, the heavens open. We worried about all the concrete we had worked on getting pitted and ruined.

"Get something," Steve shouted, scrambling to gather up his tools. I ran into the house. I couldn't find a plastic drop cloth quickly enough, so I grabbed one of my best sheets off the bed. As I watched the linen turn muddy and gray in the rain, I consoled myself. *In the future I won't care that I ruined the sheet,* I thought. *I'll just be thankful that I preserved our footprints and handprints.*

"It's our cave," Steve said of our new home. We never entertained. The zoo was our social place. Living so close by, we could have easily gotten overwhelmed, so we made it a practice never to have people over. It wasn't unfriendliness, it was simple self-preservation. Our brick residence was for our family: Steve and me, Bindi, Sui, and Shasta.

Almost as soon as we got our baby home, we packed her up to leave. Bindi was six days old when she embarked on her first film shoot (actually, her second, if you count filming her birth). Steve, Bindi, and I headed off for the United States, with a stop first at Australia's Double Island to film turtles.

We drove through the Double Island sand dunes, spending a day filming on the area's spectacular beaches. Bindi did marvelously. Some of the four-wheel driving was a bit rough, so I would lean over her capsule in the back of the four-wheel drive, helping to hold her head, so that the bouncing of the truck wouldn't jostle her around too much.

Once we arrived on location, she was absolutely content. Fraser, one of the assistants on the shoot, stayed with Bindi while Steve and I filmed. Then we'd walk around behind the camera to hug and kiss her, and I could feed her. She didn't squeak or squawk. I swear she seemed to keep quiet when John called out "Rolling!"

It felt fantastic to be back filming again, and it made me realize how much I missed it. The crew represented our extended family. I never once caught a feeling of annoyance or impatience at the prospect of having a six-day-old baby on set. To the contrary, the atmosphere was one of joy. I can mark precisely Bindi Irwin's introduction to the wonderful world of wildlife documentary filming: Thursday, July 30, 1998, in the spectacular subtropics of the Queensland coast, where the brilliant white sand meets the turquoise water. This is where the sea turtles navigate the rolling surf each year to come ashore and lay their eggs.

Next stop: America, baby on board. Bindi was so tiny she fit on an airline pillow. Steve watched over her almost obsessively, fussing with her and guarding to see if anything would fall out of the overhead bins whenever they were opened. Such a protective daddy.

Our first shoot in California focused on rattlesnakes and spiders. We got a cute photo of baby Bindi with a little hat on and a brown tarantula on her head. In Texas she got to meet toads and Trans-Pecos rat snakes. Steve found two stunning specimens of the nonvenomous snakes in an abandoned house. I watched as two-week-old Bindi reacted to their presence. She gazed up at the snakes and her small, shaky arms reached out toward them.

I laughed with delight at her eagerness.

Steve looked over at me, as if to say, *See? Our own little wildlife warrior!*

In Florida we got to hang out with some of America's finest at Eglin Air Force Base. The army Rangers there had been clearing a section of bush for doing operations and had encountered a huge eastern diamondback rattlesnake. Diamondbacks grow to be the largest rattlers anyway, but this one was big for another reason: She was pregnant. Not long after the Rangers' reptile handlers had transported her back to a holding facility, she gave birth.

We watched as the newborn rattlers worked their way out, lay still for a short moment, and then immediately began striking at everything and anything nearby. Although it was a great defense mechanism, in case a predator was about to eat them, it appeared pretty comical. Bite, bite, bite, strike, strike, strike. Then they would curl up and hide for a while. Soon enough it was back on the offensive: bite, strike, bite. They were all fang, and trying to look tough. An interesting way to greet the world.

Steve and I scooped up the baby rattlesnakes and held them until they went through their strike phase. We made sure to set them down before they went back to their frenzied biting.

"What happens if you're bitten by a venomous snake while you are breastfeeding?" Steve asked.

"I don't know," I answered. "I'd probably have to stop breastfeeding, right?"

"Just be sure not to get bitten," Steve said.

"Deal," I said. I scooped up a little wet rattler, talked to the camera, then set the snake back down. *Boing, boing, boing* went the baby rattler, jumping madly around, trying to bite everything. Even the Rangers laughed.

Once the Rangers had completed their training mission, all the dangerous wildlife they collected (including the rattlers) would go right back where they came from. We were very proud to have worked with some of America's heroes.

Steve was in his element during the Florida shoot. He spotted a coral snake at Eglin, and another huge diamondback. It was stinking hot, like most summers in the southeast. Bindi spent a lot of her time sitting in the air-conditioned vehicle, while one of the crew stayed with her. I would move far enough away so that the camera's microphone couldn't pick up the sound of the truck running, film like mad, and then run back to be with her.

Bindi always enjoyed being close to Steve. He seemed to both excite her and keep her calm at the same time. He showed her everything that entered his world, all the wildlife, the landscapes, and the people. Even at only a few weeks old, Bindi turned her head when Steve walked past her room. I don't think she could even see him, but she smelled or somehow sensed his presence. Then she fussed until he came and picked her up.

The bond between father and daughter continued to grow stronger.

As much as he influenced her, Bindi changed Steve, too. After our Florida trip, Bindi and I went home, while Steve flew off to the Indonesian island of Sumatra. We couldn't accompany him because of the malaria risk, so we kept the home fires burning instead. At one point, Steve was filming with orangutans when his newfound fatherhood came in handy.

A local park ranger who had worked with

the national park's orangutans for twenty-five years accompanied Steve into the rain forest, where they encountered a mother and baby orangutan. The rangers keep a close eye on the orangutans to prevent poaching, and the ranger recognized a lot of the animals by sight.

"She reminds me of Bindi," Steve exclaimed, seeing the infant ape. It was a mischievous, happy baby, clinging to her mother way up in the top branches of a tree.

"This will be great to film," Steve said. "I'll climb into the tree, and then you can get me and the orangutans in the same shot."

The ranger waved his hands, heading Steve off. "You absolutely can't do that," the ranger said. "The mother orangutans are extremely protective. If you make a move anywhere near that tree, she'll come down and pull your arms off."

Steve paused to listen.

"They are very strong," the ranger said. "She won't tolerate you in her tree."

"I won't climb very close to her," Steve said. "I'll just go a little way up. Then the camera can shoot up at me and get her in the background."

The ranger looked doubtful. "Okay,

Steve," he said. "But I promise you, she will come down out of that tree and pull your head off."

"Don't worry, mate," Steve said confidently, "she'll be right."

He climbed into the tree. Down came the mother, just as the ranger had predicted. Tugging, pulling, and dragging her baby along behind her, she deftly made her way right over to Steve. He didn't move. He sat on his tree limb and watched her come toward him.

The crew filmed it all, and it became one of the most incredible shots in documentary filmmaking. Mama came close to Steve. She swung onto the same tree limb. Then she edged her way over until she sat right beside him. Everyone on the crew was nervous, except for Steve.

Mama put her arm around Steve's shoulders. *I guess the ranger was right,* Steve thought, wondering if he would be armless or headless in the very immediate future. While hanging on to her baby, Mama pulled Steve in tight with her other arm, looked him square in the face, and . . . started making kissy faces at him.

The whole crew busted up laughing as

Mama puckered up her lips and looked lovingly into Steve's eyes.

"You've got a beautiful little baby, sweetheart," Steve said softly. The baby scrambled up the limb away from them, and without taking her eyes off Steve, the mother reached over, grabbed her baby, and dragged the tot back down.

"You're a good mum," Steve cooed. "You take good care of that little bib-bib."

"I have never seen anything like that," the park ranger said later. I had to believe that the encounter was further evidence of the uncanny connection Steve had with the wildlife he loved so much, as well as one proud parent recognizing another.

One day in Sumatra, Steve was climbing into the forest canopy alongside a family of orangutans when he fell. A four-inch spike of bamboo jammed into the back of his leg. As always, he was loath to go to the hospital and successfully cut the spike of bamboo out of his own leg himself.

Ever since I'd met him, Steve had refused to let me dress or have anything to do with any of his wounds. He didn't even like to talk about his injuries. I think this was a legacy from his years alone in the bush. He had his own approach to being injured, and he called it "the goanna theory."

"Sometimes you'll see a goanna that's been hurt," he said. "He may have been hit by a car and had a leg torn off. Maybe he's missing a chunk of his tail. Does he walk around feeling sorry for himself? No. He goes about his business, hunting for food, looking for mates, climbing trees, and doing the best that he can."

That's the goanna theory. Steve would take into consideration how debilitating the specific wound was, but then he would carry on. A bamboo spike in the back of his leg? Well, it hurt. But his leg still worked. He continued filming.

Meanwhile, my life back at home was made much easier with the help of Steve's sister Joy and her husband, Frank Muscillo. Tall and dark-haired, with an open, friendly face, Frank began at the zoo by working half days, helping me with payroll and paperwork. If it wasn't for Frank coming to the rescue during that period when I was trying to juggle work with a new baby, I don't know what I would have done.

Frank was family. I felt I could trust him implicitly with any money matters. He was brilliant at bookkeeping, an exceptional businessman, and a dad as well. With two kids of his own, he understood that no matter how busy work got, family came first. Eventually he became general manager of the zoo, and a vital component to its success.

Bindi, meanwhile, was blossoming. At just six weeks old, she held her head up and reached for objects. She even tried to scoot around a bit. She pushed with her little legs and worked her way across the bed. When Steve came home from Sumatra, it was obvious how much he had missed his little girl. I had to smile when Steve sat down on the couch with Bindi, telling her of his adventures moment by moment, while she stared intently at him, trying desperately to puzzle out his words.

"She really did miss you," I said.

"No, she didn't," Steve scoffed. Then he added, his face brightening hopefully, "How could you tell?"

I knew the truth. Even as a newborn, Bindi behaved differently when Steve was around. When she saw Steve come home after one of his trips, she got excited and happy and would literally quiver with joy.

Steve shared everything with her. He took her around the zoo and introduced her to the wildlife. One day he took her into the enclosure with Agro, one of our biggest crocodiles. A school group had come to the zoo, and they assembled in their neatly pressed uniforms around the enclosure. Bindi squealed with delight and looked intently at Agro. That afternoon Steve did the crocodile demonstration with his daughter cradled in his arms. The school-group visitors looked impressed and perhaps a bit jealous.

After the croc show, I noticed Bindi was as alert as I had ever seen her. She was so thrilled. Joining her daddy for the croc demo became something she looked forward to. Sometimes Bindi and I would sit in the enclosure to watch Steve with the crocodiles, and she would cry until he picked her up so she could be part of the action. *The apple doesn't fall far from the tree,* I thought.

On Bindi's first birthday in July 1999, we began a tradition of our own. We threw open the doors of the zoo with free admission to all children. We offered free birthday cake and invited cockatoos, camels, snakes, and lizards to party with us. It poured rain all day, but it didn't matter. Steve placed a giant birthday cake in front of his daughter. It could have served one hundred people, and we'd ordered up several of them for the celebration.

Bindi had never had sugar before, or any kind of dessert or lolly. She carefully took a frosting flower off the top and tasted it. Puzzlement and then joy transformed her face. She dove in headfirst. Cheers and laughter erupted from the crowd of three hundred, all of whom had shown up to celebrate.

Steve's mother, Lyn, looked on that day with a proud smile. I thought back to what it must have been like when Lyn first started the zoo. It was just a small wildlife park, with admission only forty cents for adults and twenty cents for kids. Now it was an expanding enterprise, part of an ambitious conservation effort and a complement to our wildlife documentaries. But her son's favorite job was still the humble one of being Dad. I could read on Lyn's face how important it was to her that Steve had started a family. And Bindi had a great day wearing a small pink sweater that her gran had made for her.

That night Bindi, Steve, and I all curled up in bed together. “As long as we’re together,” Steve said, “everything will be just fine.”

It was spooky, and I didn’t want to think about it, but it did indeed seem that Steve got into trouble more when he was off on his own. Around that time, on a shoot in Africa with the bushmen of the Kalahari Desert, Steve slipped as he rushed to get a shot of a lizard. He put his hand out to catch himself, and placed it down right in the middle of a euphorbia plant. The bush broke into pieces, and the splinters sank deep into Steve’s hand.

Kalahari bushmen use the resin of the euphorbia plant to poison-tip their spears. Steve’s arm swelled and turned black. He became feverish and debated whether to go home or to the hospital. He sought the advice of the bushmen who worked with the poisonous resin regularly.

“What do you do if you get nailed by this poison?”

The bushmen smiled broadly. “We die,” they said.

John filmed every step of the way as the

skin of Steve's arm continued to blacken and he rode out the fever. He worried about the residual effects of gangrene.

Ultimately, Steve survived, but he felt the effects for weeks afterward. Once again, Steve and I discussed how uneasy we felt when we were apart. Every time we were together on a trip, we knew we'd be okay. When we were apart, though, we shared a disconcerting feeling that was hard to put into words. It made me feel hollow inside.

The Africa trip had taken Steve away from us for three weeks, and Bindi had changed so much while he was away. We agreed that we would never be apart from Bindi and that at least one of us would always be with her. I just felt bad for Steve that I had been the lucky one for the past three weeks. He missed her so much.

The next documentary would be different. We were taking a DC-10 all the way across the country, from the east coast to the west. Together we flew into the Red Centre, the interior of the continent and the location of Ayers Rock—one of Australia's most recognizable icons.

"Have a look at it," Steve said when we arrived. "It's the heart of Australia."

I could see why. A huge red mountain rose up out of the flat, sandy landscape. The rock appeared out of place in the great expanse of the desert. The Aborigines knew it as Uluru, and they preferred that tourists did not clamber over their sacred site.

We respectfully filmed only the areas we were allowed to access with the local Aborigines' blessing. As we approached the rock, Steve saw a lizard nearby. He turned to the camera to talk about it. I was concentrating on Steve, Steve was concentrating on the lizard, and John was filming. Bindi was with us, and she could barely take two steps on her own at this point, so I knew I could afford to watch Steve.

But after John called out, "Got it," and we turned back to Bindi, we were amazed at what we saw. Bindi was leaning against the base of Ayers Rock. She had placed both her palms against the smooth stone, gently put her cheek up to the rock, and stood there, mesmerized.

"She's listening," Steve whispered. It was an eerie moment. The whole crew stopped and stared. Then Bindi suddenly seemed to come out of her trance. She plopped down and started stuffing the red sand of Uluru into her mouth like it was delicious.

We also filmed a thorny devil busily licking up ants from the sandy soil. The one-of-a-kind lizard is covered with big, lumpy, bumpy scales and spikes.

"When it rains," Steve told the camera, "the water droplets run along its body and end up channeling over its face, so that if there is any rain at all, the thorny devil can get a drink without having to look for water!"

It's a pity she won't remember any of it, I thought, watching Bindi crouch down to examine the thorny devil's tongue as it madly ate ants. But we had the photos and the footage. *What a lucky little girl,* I thought. *We'll have all these special experiences recorded for her to take out and enjoy anytime she wants to remember.*

Our life proceeded in stages. Steve traveled to East Timor to film. The Australian Diggers had contacted us about a captive crocodile that needed our help. At the time, the country was at war, so Steve had to tackle the project without Bindi and me. But I knew that for the next trip, we would be together as a family.

First I had planned a visit to Oregon; then Steve would join us after Bindi and I promoted our new Crocodile Hunter toy line at the big annual toy fair in New York City. Being on the road together was stacks of fun. We'd jump in a hotel tub bubble bath, order room service, and eat breakfast in bed. Traveling with Steve always meant there'd be loads of adventures.

So Bindi and I flew to the United States ahead of Steve. We drove down to the Oregon coast, where my sister and I share a small beach cabin. We couldn't contact Steve because mobile phones weren't in range. There was no phone at the cabin, either, only a pay phone across the street at a gas station. It was one of the rare periods when we were out of touch for days at a time.

During this time, Steve's parents had decided to move closer to us at the zoo. They would manage our property on the Great Dividing Range, which we'd named Ironbark Station. Lyn was particularly thrilled about being closer to the family. She and Bob had been living in Rosedale, on the Queensland coast, a four-and-a-half-hour drive from the zoo. Ironbark Station was only two hours away.

We'd purchased conservation land over a period of many years, and we were attempting to restore the native bush. We began planting eucalypts not long after we bought the property. First we planted dozens, then hundreds, and finally thousands. Steve worked into the night planting trees. If the rain didn't come immediately, he would dutifully water each and every seedling. We had high hopes that one day the land would offer refuge to everything from koalas to phascogales.

"It will take a lifetime to establish these trees," he said. "But one day they will be big, they will have hollows, and there will be a place where animals can live again." Even in its raw, cattle-ravaged state, the land was heaven. The rufous bettongs were out in force every night, and the white-winged choughs flew down to keep an eye on us wherever we worked.

We had pieced together land parcels for a total of six hundred and fifty acres. This was the property Lyn and Bob were taking over in 1999.

I was sound asleep at the Oregon beach

cabin one night when there was a knock at the door. A woman who said she was from the Red Cross stood on the front porch. I was foggy-headed. At first, I could not get through my brain what she was saying.

"I don't mean to alarm you," she said. "But you need to call home immediately."

Terror struck me. My mind raced. Where was Steve? Bindi lay asleep in the bedroom. I asked the woman from the Red Cross to stay on the porch while I went across the street to the pay phone. The international calling procedure seemed immensely complicated that morning, and terribly slow. I tried to keep my fingers steady as I dialed.

The sun had not yet risen. I was in my robe. It was February of 2000, and I remember thinking, *It's always the coldest just before the sun comes up.*

I heard Steve's voice on the other end of the phone and experienced an immediate flood of relief. *He's alive.* But something was terribly wrong. Steve was incoherent. I couldn't figure out what had happened.

Not long before, we had lost our favorite crocodile to old age, and I thought that something had happened to one of our animals. But the tone of Steve's voice was different. He was sobbing, but finally managed to choke out the words.

His mother had been killed in a car accident.

I felt the blood drain from my face. I couldn't believe it. I didn't know what he was talking about. He tried to explain, but he couldn't really talk. The next thing I knew, the line went dead.

It took a few frantic calls to find out what had happened. In the process of moving to their new home on our property, Lyn had left Rosedale to make one last trip with a few remaining family possessions. She was driving with the family malamute, Aylic, in the passenger seat beside her, and Sharon, their bird-eating spider, in a glass terrarium tank in the back of the truck. Lyn left the Rosedale house early, about three o'clock in the morning.

As she approached Ironbark Station, her Ute left the road traveling sixty miles an hour. The truck hit a tree and she died instantly. Aylic was killed as well, and the tank holding the bird-eating spider was smashed to pieces.

Early in the morning, at the precise moment when the crash happened, Steve was working on the backhoe at the zoo. He suddenly felt as if he had been hit by something that knocked him over, and he fell violently off the machine, hitting the ground so hard that his sunglasses came off. He told me later that he knew something terrible had happened.

Steve got in his Ute and started driving. He had no idea what had happened, but he knew where he had to go. It was still early. With uncanny precision, he drove toward where the accident occurred. His mobile phone rang. It was Frank. When his brother-in-law told him what had happened and where, Steve realized he was already headed there.

I immediately packed up Bindi and went to catch the next plane home. The family was in free fall. Steve was in shock, and Bob was even worse off. Lyn had always acted as the matriarch, the one who kept everything together. She was such a strong figure, a leader. Her death didn't seem real.

I sat on that plane and looked down at Bindi. *Life is changed forever now,* I thought. As we arrived home, I didn't know what to expect. I had never dealt with grief like this before. Lyn was only in her fifties, and it seemed cruel to have her life cut short, as she was on the brink of a dream she had held in her heart forever. These were going to be her golden years. She and Bob could embark on the life they had worked so hard to achieve. They would be together, near their family, where they could take care of the land and enjoy the wildlife they loved.

I couldn't imagine what Steve, his dad, and his sisters were going through. My heart was broken. Bindi's gran was gone just when they had most looked forward to spending time together. The aftermath of Lyn's death was every bit as awful as I could have imagined. Steve was absolutely inconsolable, and Bob was very obviously unable to cope. Joy and Mandy were trying to keep things together, but they were distraught and heartbroken. Everyone at the zoo was somber. I felt I needed to do something, yet I felt helpless, sad, and lost.

Steve's younger sister Mandy performed the mournful task of sifting through the smashed items from the truck. One of the objects Lyn had packed was Bob's teapot. There was nothing Bob enjoyed more than a cup of tea. As Mandy went to wash out the teapot, she noticed movement. Inside was Sharon, the bird-eating spider, the sole survivor of the accident. Although her tank had been smashed to bits, she had managed to crawl into the teapot to hide.

After the funeral, time appeared to slow down and then stop entirely. Steve talked about moving out to Ironbark Station. He couldn't seem to order his thoughts. He no longer saw a reason for going on with all the projects on which we had worked so hard. Bindi was upset but didn't have the understanding to know why. She was too young to get her head around what had happened. She simply cried when she saw her daddy crying.

It would be a long time before life returned to anything like normalcy. Lyn's death was something that Steve would never truly overcome. His connection with his mum, like that of so many mothers and sons, was unusually close. Lyn Irwin was a pioneer in wildlife rehabilitation work. She had given her son a great legacy, and eventually that gift would win out over death. But in the wake of her accident, all we could see was loss.

Steve headed out into the bush alone, with just Sui and his swag. He reverted to his youth, to his solitary formative years. But grief trailed him. My heart broke for my husband. I was not sure he would ever find his way back.

CHAPTER FOURTEEN

Coming Back

When the going gets hard, sometimes the best you can do is be there for people. All I wanted was to make things better, but this was something I just couldn't fix. I didn't know if I should dwell on what had happened or focus on the future. This was the dilemma I faced with Steve after Lyn's death. I so much wanted to turn back the clock, but there was no way I could.

Steve coped by throwing himself into working on the land. Up on the driver's seat of a backhoe or a bulldozer, he could be alone with his thoughts. He worked the property around the zoo to prepare it for expansion. His idea was to create a mini-Madagascar, an island habitat for the zoo. We would develop a magical island with giant land tortoises, and the trees above filled with lemurs.

True to his ideal of getting wildlife into people's hearts, Steve thought zoo visitors shouldn't have to stare across the water at the animals. They would take a boat ride to adventure and disembark among land tortoises and lemurs. If the lemurs felt like coming down to play, they could. If they wanted to stay up in the trees, they could do that, too. The island would be a place where they would roam free.

Using heavy equipment, Steve carved away at our property just beyond what was then the northern boundary of the zoo. There would be a cheetah run here also, and space for a new hospital for rescued wildlife. But watching him work an excavator from afar, I felt like Steve wasn't thinking about the future so much as trying to cope with the immediate past.

Just then Hollywood came calling. If you could design a place as far removed as possible from the real-life questions of grief and loss, Hollywood would be it. No one really noticed that it was an emotionally scarred Steve who showed up at the Daytime Emmy Awards ceremony that year.

Most of them were too busy with their own problems to worry about anyone else's.

Croc Files was a fun show, with each episode taking kids on a new adventure with stacks of exciting wildlife. It had been nominated in the category of Outstanding Children's Series. The awards were held in May 2000 at the Century Plaza in Los Angeles.

The hustle and bustle of the Emmys didn't impress Steve much. In his present frame of mind, he was loath to go anywhere. The big city wasn't where Steve wanted to be, even in the best of times, and now it was even harder because he would never again be able to share his achievements with his mum.

As it happened, the night belonged to Disney Channel's *Bill Nye, the Science Guy,* which took home a total of four Emmys, including the one for Outstanding Children's Series. I felt badly for John Stainton and Judi Bailey who, as producers of *Croc Files,* would have been the ones actually receiving the award. I felt it was a big deal to be nominated at all.

Hollywood wasn't through with us yet.

We entered into initial exploratory talks

with MGM, one of the major Hollywood studios, about doing a Crocodile Hunter movie.

Gearing up to film a movie would prove to be completely different from packing up and going bush to film a documentary. So much work goes on behind the scenes before the cameras roll: contracts, logistics, script development, and budgeting. In spring 2000, we were still in the who, what, when, where, and how phases of filming a movie. We were nowhere near actually knuckling down to do it. Although the negotiations were tedious, conducted in rooms full of Hollywood heavy hitters, Steve never wavered in his conviction that the movie would have a strong conservation message.

He convinced John Stainton to agree that there would be no CGI (computer-generated imagery) wildlife in the movie. We didn't want to pretend to react to an animal in front of a green screen, and then have computer graphic technicians complete the shot later. That was how Hollywood would normally have done it, but that wasn't an option for Steve.

"All the animals have to be real," he insisted to the executives at MGM. "I'm doing all of my own stunts. Otherwise, I am not interested."

I always believed that Steve would excel at anything he put his mind to, and a movie would be no different. The camera loved him. As talks ground on at MGM, we came up with a title: *Crocodile Hunter: Collision Course*. But mostly we had phone calls and meetings.

The main sticking point was that no insurance company would touch us. No underwriter would write a policy for a project that required Steve to be working with real live crocodiles.

As negotiations seemed to be grinding to a halt, we were all feeling frustrated. Steve looked around at John, Judi, and the others. He could see that everybody had gotten a bit stretched on all our various projects. He decided we needed a break.

He didn't lead us into the bush this time. Instead, Steve said a magic word. "Samoa."

"Sea snakes?" I asked.

"Surfing," he said. He planned a ten-day shoot for a surfing documentary.

Steve loved surfing almost as much as he loved wildlife. The pounding his body had taken playing rugby, wrestling crocs, and doing heavy construction at the zoo had left him with problem knees and a bad shoulder. He felt his time tackling some of the biggest surf might be nearing an end.

In Samoa, Steve didn't spend just a few hours out in the waves. He would be out there twelve to fourteen hours a day. I didn't surf, but I was awestruck at Steve's ability to stare down the face of a wave that was as high as a building. He had endurance beyond any surfer I had ever seen. Steve had a support boat nearby, so he could swim over, get hydrated, or grab a protein bar. But that was it. He didn't stop for lunch. He would eat breakfast, surf all day, and then eat a big dinner.

I knew this was the best therapy for him. Surfing at Boulders was downright dangerous, but Steve reveled in the challenge. He surfed with Wes, his best mate in the world. I sat on a rocky point with my eye glued to the camera so I wouldn't miss a single wave. While Bindi gathered shells and played on the beach under her nanny's watchful eye, I admired Steve with his long arms and broad shoulders, powerfully paddling onto wave after wave.

Not even the Pacific Ocean with its most

powerful sets could slow him down. He caught the most amazing barrels I have ever seen, and carved up the waves with such ferocity that I didn't want the camera to miss a single moment.

On the beach in Samoa, while Bindi helped her dad wax his board, I caught a glimpse of joy in eyes that had been so sad.

Along with John and Judi, we took a big risk and started filming on the movie before we had a contract signed with MGM. There didn't seem to be any choice. I imagined all the insurance underwriters across the world reacting to the phrase "live crocodiles." Those two words would be enough to blow them right out of their cubicles. So we began shooting with our zoo crocodiles, but without signatures on the dotted line for the movie.

A particular scene in the script—and a good example of an insurance man's nightmare—had a crocodile trying to lunge into a boat. Only Steve's expertise could make this happen, since the action called for Steve and me to be in the boat at the time. If the lunging crocodile happened to hook his head over the edge of the boat, he would tip us both into the water. That would be a one-way trip.

"How are you going to work it?" I asked Steve.

"Get the crocs accustomed to the dinghy first," he said. "Then I'll see if I can get them interacting with me while I'm in the boat."

First he tried Agro, one of our biggest male crocs. Agro was too wary of the boat. He's a smart crocodile. I think he remembered back when he was captured. He didn't want any of it. We decided to try with our friend Charlie.

Charlie had been very close to ending up at a farm, his skin turned into boots, bags, and belts. He definitely had attitude. He spent a lot of his time trying to kill everything within range. Steve felt good about the possibility of Charlie having a go.

Because he was filming a movie and not shooting a documentary, John had a more complex setup than usual, utilizing three thirty-five-millimeter cameras. Each one would film in staggered succession, so that the film magazine changes would never happen all at once. There would never be a time when film was not rolling. We couldn't very well ask a crocodile to wait while a fresh mag was loaded into a camera.

"You need to be careful to stay out of Charlie's line of sight," Steve said to me. "I want Charlie focusing only on me. If he changes focus and starts attacking you, it's going to be too difficult for me to control the situation."

Right. Steve got no argument from me. Getting anywhere near those bone-crushing jaws was the furthest thing from my mind. I wasn't keen on being down on the water with a huge saltwater crocodile trying to get me. I would have to totally rely on Steve to keep me safe.

We stepped into the dinghy, which was moored in Charlie's enclosure, secured front and back with ropes. Charlie came over immediately to investigate. It didn't take much to encourage him to have a go at Steve. Steve grabbed a top-jaw rope. He worked on roping Charlie while the cameras rolled.

Time and time again, Charlie hurled himself straight at Steve, a half ton of reptile flesh exploding up out of the water a few feet away from me. I tried to hang on precariously and keep the boat counterbalanced. I didn't want Steve to lose his footing and topple in. Charlie was one angry crocodile. He would have loved nothing more than to get his teeth into Steve.

As Charlie used his powerful tail to propel himself out of the water, he arched his neck and opened his jaws wide, whipping his head back and forth, snapping and gnashing. Steve carefully threw the top-jaw rope, but he didn't actually want to snag Charlie. Then he would have had to get the rope off without stressing the croc, and that would have been tricky.

The cameras rolled. Charlie lunged. I cowered. Steve continued to deftly toss the rope. Then, all of a sudden, Charlie swung at the rope instead of Steve, and the rope went right over Charlie's top jaw. A perfect toss, provided that had been what Steve was trying to do. But it wasn't. We had a roped croc on our hands that we really didn't want.

Steve immediately let the rope go slack. Charlie had it snagged in his teeth. Because of Steve's quick thinking and prompt maneuvering, the rope came clear. We breathed a collective sigh of relief.

Steve looked up at the cameras. "I think you've got it."

John agreed. “I think we do, mate.”

The crew cheered. The shoot lasted several minutes, but in the boat, I wasn’t sure if it had been seconds or hours. Watching Steve work Charlie up close had been amazing—a huge, unpredictable animal with a complicated thought process, able to outwit its prey, an animal that had been on the planet for millions of years, yet Steve knew how to manipulate him and got some fantastic footage.

To the applause of the crew, Steve got us both out of the boat. He gave me a big hug. He was happy. This was what he loved best, being able to interact and work with wildlife. Never before had anything like it been filmed in any format, much less on thirty-five-millimeter film for a movie theater. We accomplished the shot with the insurance underwriters none the wiser.

Steve wanted to portray crocs as the powerful apex predators that they were, keeping everyone safe while he did it. Never once did he want it to appear as though he were dominating the crocodile, or showing off by being in close proximity to it. He wished for the crocodile to be the star of the show, not himself.

I was proud of him that day. The shoot represented Steve Irwin at his best, his true colors, and his desire to make people understand how amazing these animals are, to be witnessed by audiences in movie theaters all over the world. We filmed many more sequences with crocs, and each time Steve performed professionally and perfected the shots. He was definitely in his element.

With the live-croc footage behind us, the insurance people came on board, and we were finally able to sign a contract with MGM. We were to start filming in earnest. First stop: the Simpson Desert, with perentie lizards and fierce snakes.

The day before we headed out was an unusually warm day. Shasta had a hard time of it. Bindi wrapped her in wet towels to help her cool off. Every few minutes she would raise her head and bark a bit.

The last couple of years, Shasta's back had been out so bad that I would wheelbarrow her around. She always liked sleeping in the car. I think it made her excited to be going on a trip. That night she seemed so restless that I put her in the car and kissed her good night. I knew she'd be happiest there.

In the morning, we were off to our first official day of filming the movie. Steve put the last few things together in the zoo. I went out to get Shasta organized for staying with a friend. She was still asleep.

"Good morning, lazybones," I said. I bent down to give her a kiss on the forehead. Then I realized she wasn't there. Sometime during the night, Shasta had died. She was seventeen and a half years old, the only dog I ever had. She went through nine months of quarantine to join me in Australia. She had been a loyal friend and an excellent guard dog.

Bindi and I said good-bye to Shasta together. We discussed the circle of life and collected a few of Shasta's favorite things. She would be buried with her favorite blanket. I knew I'd never have another dog. Now Sui was the only dog in the family.

That Thanksgiving, while we were still in production with our own movie, Steve filmed a cameo appearance in Eddie Murphy's movie *Dr. Dolittle 2*.

It was a fun scene. Steve plays himself,

and Eddie plays Dolittle. Although it was shot in Los Angeles, supposedly the two of them are in the bush, and Steve is explaining how to wrangle a gator.

"I am here with Dr. Dolittle, who can actually talk with animals," Steve says. "We're here about to capture this alligator right behind us. The way to hang on to him is to grab him like this. . . ."

Meanwhile, though, the alligator has ideas of his own. In an outrageous Aussie accent, he clues Eddie in: "What I'm doing is letting Steve think I don't hear him. When he comes for me, I'm gonna turn around, and Bob's your uncle, snap his arm off!"

"Steve," Eddie says, "I think he knows we're here."

"Quiet," says Steve. "I don't want to spoil the element of surprise."

He leaps at the alligator, who snaps him up into its jaws. "Crikey!" Steve yells. "Me arm!"

Steve took people at their own merits. He was not overwhelmed or overly impressed by anybody for their star quality. It didn't matter if it was the publican in Windorah or a movie star in Los Angeles. He reacted to people as individuals.

"I liked Eddie," he said, when I asked him how the shoot went. "He's a talented man, very professional, and easy to work with."

But after spending a few days in Eddie Murphy's world, Steve pondered how the man coped with being constantly in the limelight. It was unending for Murphy. People wanted a piece of him all the time—a photograph, an autograph, a few words. Steve wondered how someone could lead a life like that. With more and more viewers in the States tuning in to Animal Planet, he was about to find out.

I think that's why Steve felt so grounded living in Australia. The population of the country is twenty million, spread over an area the size of the United States. There are still plenty of places in the vast Australian wilderness where he could get away from it all, places where he could drive for days without seeing another person. Although Steve understood the importance of working and filming in America, he always swore he would never leave his home in Australia.

Ironically enough, when we returned to the zoo, the *Dr. Dolittle* cameo almost came true. We had to transfer a big female crocodile named Toolakea to another enclosure.

Steve geared up for the move as he always did.

"Don't think about catching Toolakea," he instructed his crew, me included, before we ever got near to the enclosure. "If you're concentrating on catching her, she'll know it. We'll never get a top-jaw rope on. Crocs know when they're being hunted."

For millions of years, wild animals have evolved to use every sense to tune into the world around them. Steve understood that their survival depended on it. So as I approached the enclosure, I thought of mowing the lawn, or doing the croc show, or picking hibiscus flowers to feed the lizards. Anything but catching Toolakea.

It went like clockwork. Steve top-jaw-roped Toolakea, and we all jumped her. He decided that since she was only a little more than nine feet long, we would be able to just lift her over the fence and carry her to her other enclosure.

Steve never built his enclosures with gates. He knew that sooner or later, someone could make a mistake and not latch a gate properly. We had to be masters at fence jumping. He picked up Toolakea around her shoulders with her neck held firmly against his upper arm. This would protect his face if she started struggling. The rest of us backed him up and helped to lift Toolakea over the fence.

All of a sudden she exploded, twisting and writhing in everyone's arms.

"Down, down, down," Steve shouted. That was our signal to pin the crocodile again before picking her up. Not everyone reacted quickly enough. As Steve moved to the ground, the people on the tail were still standing up. That afforded Toolakea the opportunity to twist her head around and grab hold of Steve's thigh.

The big female croc sank her teeth deep into his flesh. I never realized it until later. Steve didn't flinch. He settled the crocodile on the ground, keeping her eyes covered to quiet her down. We lifted her again. This time she cleared the fence easily. I noticed the blood trickling down Steve's leg.

We got to the other enclosure before I asked what had happened, and he showed me. There were a dozen tears in the fabric of his khaki shorts. A half dozen of Toolakea's teeth had gotten through to his flesh, putting a number of puncture holes in his upper thigh.

As usual, Steve didn't bother with the wound. He cleaned it out and carried on, but even after his leg had healed, he couldn't feel the temperature accurately on his leg. Once, about a month after the incident, I got a drink out of the fridge and rested it on his thigh.

"I can feel something there," he said.

"Hot or cold?" I quizzed.

"I don't know," he said.

The croc-torn khaki shorts he wore that day made an amazing souvenir for a lucky sponsor of the zoo. People who donated a certain amount of money to our conservation efforts received a bonus in return: one of Steve's uniforms and a photograph of him in it. Steve was very proud to include his khakis with teeth holes in them as the gift for a generous supporter.

Steve always had a feeling that he wouldn't live a long life. He would sometimes say that he hoped a croc wouldn't get him, because he felt it would undo all of his hard work convincing people that crocs are wonderful animals worth protecting. After losing his mother, Steve seemed even more focused on accomplishing as much as possible in the time he had here on earth. He was convinced that when it was his time to go, it would be quick, as his mum had died in the car accident.

Steve didn't fear death. Maybe that was part of his secret for being so gifted with wildlife. He had such perfect love for every animal, and especially crocodiles, that there didn't seem to be any room left over for fear.

But this didn't mean that Steve didn't have his share of close calls.

One day I was feeding Cookie, Wes was feeding Mary, and our crew member Jan was backing up Wes. Steve talked to the zoo visitors about our big male, Agro, partially submerged in the water near Steve.

Steve was so intent on getting his message across about crocodiles that he might have been a bit distracted. It had poured rain that day, leaving the grass wet and slippery. Agro took full advantage when Steve's back was to the water. He powered forward like a missile, out of the water and halfway up the bank. As he came out, Wes yelled.

Agro had Steve backed against the fence. Steve couldn't move. I looked across the enclosure and saw the look on Steve's face—it wasn't fear, it was resolve. A big male saltwater croc was about to grab him. But for some unknown reason, Agro hesitated for a split second. Maybe he just couldn't believe his luck. Or he was distracted by Wes, running over to save his best friend.

Steve darted sideways and ran down the fence line. He was safe. The audience erupted in excited chatter. "Nothing short of a miracle," a crowd member said about Steve's escape. Was it? Was it his sixth sense? Was it his mate, Wes?

That night we lay in bed and I stroked his face, tracing the lines that were starting to form around the corners of his eyes, waiting for his breathing to become more regular as he fell asleep. "I thought for a minute there he had me," Steve said softly in the dark.

Steve was never one to panic, and that kind of levelheaded thinking allowed him to return the favor to Wes in a much closer call during cyclone season in March 2001. All day a massive low-pressure system lay off the coast of Queensland. The daylight took on a yellowish cast. By four o'clock that afternoon, the rain started.

Steve contacted all the staff. He told anyone who was not working outside with the animals to go home, including the accounts division, marketing staff, and web team. At four fifteen, Steve announced an official storm watch, which meant that all staff who remained needed to prepare for the potential of a flood.

During a storm, we needed to check fences. As water flowed through the enclosures at the zoo, it would push debris up against the fences, putting pressure on them that they were not designed to resist. With enough pressure from floodwaters, the fences would give, releasing the crocs and other animals from their enclosures.

By four thirty, Steve announced that the situation had escalated from "storm watch" to "cyclone watch." Bindi had been walking by my side. She wasn't quite three years old, and by now the floodwaters were already up to her chest. I carried her back to the compound.

"I'll be right back!" I shouted at Steve. He didn't hear me. The winds howled, and a deluge broke from the sky.

Our house was located on high ground. I got Bindi back home safely with her nanny, Thelma, and then I rushed back into the zoo.

All the water courses in the zoo were designed with storm grates. Steve had opened them to let the water through. Now it was time to divide the staff into teams to quickly remove debris from the bulging fences.

Animals in areas where the flooding was severe had to be moved. We shuffled the kangaroos to high ground and put the dingoes in special night quarters. We checked Harriet and the other giant tortoises to make sure they had lumbered up to the top part of their enclosures, out of the rushing water.

Twilight was upon us. Soon it would be dark, making everything we did twice as difficult. The rain came down like a waterfall, and the winds were absolutely deafening.

As darkness descended upon the zoo, we found it impossible to keep our equipment dry. The first to fail were the radios. Our walkie-talkies were now useless. We broke into smaller groups. The next to go were the torches. Even lights that were designed for use in water were succumbing to the rain. I saw some of our staff wearing head torches that sputtered and blinked off.

I teamed up with Rebecca, one of the staff from education who had volunteered to stay and help. We cleared debris from the dingo enclosure. Although the dingoes were safely locked in their warm and dry night quarters, we wanted to make sure that their fence line didn't buckle and need repair the next day.

We posted ourselves along the fence. Wading through waist-deep rushing water, we cleared armloads of leaves, sticks, and debris. Some of the ornamental rocks in the enclosure were completely submerged, and it became hard to keep our bearings with deep water covering everything.

Our efforts were fine for the enclosures that were empty or had harmless native wildlife in them such as the kangaroos. But there were several enclosures where it was a matter of security not to let the fences buckle. The number one priority were the croc enclosures. If a fence buckled and a crocodile floated loose, everyone working in the zoo would be in jeopardy.

The storm wasn't an entirely new situation. The zoo flooded almost every year. But this storm was horrendous. The chaos was illuminated by lightning flashes, as well as the spotlights from vehicles the staff had parked nearby, trying to keep the work areas visible.

The enclosure next to the dingoes held Graham the crocodile. Wes, Steve, and other staff battled the flood in Graham's home. One man stood on the fence to spot the croc. He had to shout to Wes and Steve as they cleared the fence line inside the enclosure in waist-deep, dark waters. With the vehicle spotlights casting weird shadows, he had to scope out the murky water and try to discern the crocodile from among the floating bits of debris.

Once the backup man had the crocodile pegged, he kept a close eye on him. If Graham submerged, Wes and Steve had to be warned immediately. The spotter worked hard to keep a bead on Graham. Steve and Wes were synchronized with their every move. They had worked together like this for years. They didn't even have to speak to each other to communicate.

There was no room for error as the amount of time spent in Graham's enclosure was kept to a minimum. They jumped into the enclosure, cleared one, two, three armloads of debris, then jumped back out and re-evaluated the situation.

Graham's fence line had a bow in it, but it wasn't in any danger of buckling. Steve and Wes were doing a good job, and there was no need for me to be there with them. It was more urgent for me to keep the dingo fence line intact next door.

Graham's female, named Bindi, was nesting, and this added another dangerous dimension to the job, since Graham was feeling particularly protective. The men were also keenly aware that nighttime meant croc time—and Graham would be stalking them with real intent.

They reached down for their three armloads of debris. Steve scooped up his first load, flung it out, and gathered his second. Suddenly, Wes slammed into the fence with such force that his body was driven in an arc right over the top of Steve.

It only took a split second for Steve to realize what had happened. As Wes had bent over to reach for an armload of debris, he had been hit from behind by more than twelve feet of reptile, weighing close to nine hundred pounds.

Graham grabbed Wes, his top teeth sinking into Wes's bum, his bottom teeth hooking into the back of Wes's thigh, just above his knee. The croc then closed his mouth, exerting that amazing three thousand pounds per square inch of jaw pressure, pulling and tearing tissue as he did.

The croc hit violently. Wes instinctively twisted away and rolled free of Graham's jaws, but two fist-sized chunks were torn from his backside. The croc instantly swung in for another grab. Wes pushed the lunging croc's head away, but not before Graham's teeth crushed through his finger. They crashed back down into the water. Wes screamed out when he was grabbed, but no one could hear him because of the roar of the storm.

In almost total darkness, Steve seized a pick handle that rested near the fence. He turned toward the croc as Graham was lining Wes up for another bite. Wes was on his side now, in water that was about three feet deep. He could see the crocodile in the lights of a Ute spotlight that shone over the murk—the dark outline of the osteodermal plates along the crocodile's back.

As Graham moved in, Wes knew the next bite would be to his skull. It would be all over. Wes braced himself for the inevitable, but it didn't come.

Steve reached into the water and grabbed Graham's back legs. He didn't realize that Graham had released Wes in preparation for that final bite. He thought Graham was holding Wes under the water. Steve pulled with all his strength, managing to turn the crocodile around to focus on him.

As Graham lunged toward Steve, Steve drove the pick handle into the crocodile's mouth and started hammering at his head. Wes saw what was happening and scrambled up the fence.

"I'm out mate, I'm out," Wes yelled, blood pouring down his leg.

Steve looked up to see Wes on the top of the fence. He realized that even though Wes was wounded, he was poised to jump back down into the water to try to rescue his best mate.

"Get out," Steve shouted. "I'm all right." Wes scrambled over the fence as the croc turned again to grab Steve. Steve and Wes both toppled over the fence and crashed down.

In the dim light, Steve could see how badly Wes had been torn open. "Mate, I'll give you a hand," Steve said. "Let me carry you back to the compound."

"It's okay!" Wes yelled through the downpour. "I can make it myself." Both men pushed their way through the water toward the compound. No one else even knew what had happened. We continued working in the rain.

Somehow Frank got word to the dingo enclosure. "You'd better get to the compound," came the message. "Graham grabbed Wes."

I felt cold chills go down my arms into my fingers. Graham was a large enough crocodile that he could easily kill prey the size of a man. I struggled through the water toward the compound. *This is a nightmare,* I thought. It felt like a bad dream, trying desperately to run in the waist-deep water, and yet feeling like I was in slow motion, struggling my way forward.

When I got to the compound, I was shocked. Wes was conscious and standing up. I had a look at his wounds. The gaping holes torn out of his bottom and the back of his leg were horrifying. Both wounds were bigger than my fist. He was badly torn up.

We discussed whether or not to call an

ambulance, and then decided we would take Wes to the hospital ourselves. Wes was fluctuating between feeling euphorically happy to be alive and lashing out in anger. He was going into shock and had lost a lot of blood.

Steve drove. A trip that would normally have taken half an hour took less than twenty minutes. The emergency room was having a busy night. By now Wes's face was somewhere between pale and gray—the pain was well and truly setting in. We explained to a nurse that he needed help immediately, but because we had a blanket over him to keep him warm, the severity of his injuries didn't really hit home.

Finally the nurse peeked under the blanket. She gasped. Wes was so terribly injured, I was worried that he would still bleed out.

Steve and I were both very emotional. So many thoughts went through our heads. Why Wes? Why hadn't Steve been grabbed? What kind of chance was it that Graham had grabbed Wes in probably the only manner that would not have killed him instantly?

We realized again how much we loved

Wes. The thought that we almost lost him terrified us. It was a horrible, emotional Friday night. Over the course of the weekend we learned that Wes would probably make a full recovery. He would keep his leg and probably regain most movement. There was still some doubt as to whether he was going to need skin grafts.

Steve laid his life on the line to defend Wes. And as severely injured as Wes was, he stopped at the top of the fence to turn back and help Steve. That was mateship; that was love. It made me think of the line from scripture: *Greater love hath no man than this, that a man lay down his life for his friends.* Steve and Wes were lucky, for they were truly friends.

We lost not a single animal that night. Every last duck, koala, and roo turned up fine, healthy, and accounted for.

After three months, as Wes's wounds healed up completely, Steve went to him with a proposition. "What do you reckon, Wes," he said, "are you up for a board meeting?"

They grabbed their surfboards, and we all headed to the Fiji Islands. Tavarua was an exclusive atoll, beautiful, with great surf. Steve and Wes also surfed Namotu and caught some unbelievable waves.

One day the face of the waves coming in had to have been sixteen feet plus. Just paddling out to the break was epic. I didn't realize how much effort it took until we had a guest with us, a young lady from Europe who was a mad keen surfer.

Steve paddled out to catch some waves, and she paddled out after him. After several minutes, it became apparent that she was having trouble. We idled the boat closer and pulled her in. She collapsed in complete exhaustion. The current had been so strong that, even paddling as hard as she could, she was able only to hold her own in the water.

I tried to photograph Steve from the boat. Peter, the captain, very obligingly ran up the side of the wave exactly at the break. I had a great side angle of Steve as he caught each wave. But the whole process scared me. The boat rose up, up, up on the massive swell. As the green water of the crest started to lip over the boat, we crashed over the top, smashed into the back of the wave, and slid down the other side.

"It's okay," I yelled to Captain Peter.

"What?" he shouted, unable to hear as the boat pounded through the swell. "What's okay?"

I gestured back toward the shore. "I don't need such . . . incredibly . . . good . . . shots," I stuttered.

I just wasn't confident enough to take photographs while surfing in a boat. I decided to be more of a beach bunny, filming beach breaks or shooting the surfing action from the safety and stability of the shoreline.

But even on dry land, the rug was about to be pulled out from under us again.

CHAPTER FIFTEEN

Baby Bob

After the storm and Wes's accident, we re-evaluated the safety procedures at the zoo. But the circumstances had been so unusual that night, there wasn't anything we could have done differently. Wes wore the spectacular scars from Graham's attack.

The bond between Wes and Steve only grew stronger. I don't think there is a similar concept in the rest of the world as the traditional Australian ideal of "mateship." "Best friends" just doesn't do it. Mateship is deeper. It's someone who has your back, always and forever. If there's a storm coming in on the horizon, your first thought is, *I wonder how the heavy weather is going to affect my best mate?* Your thoughts go to him no matter what happens.

That's how it was with Wes and Steve. Wes started working at the zoo when he was fourteen and Steve was already in his twenties. Wes backed him up on croc captures. It was a friendship tested and retested in the bush. Through the years both men had numerous opportunities to save each other's lives. But nothing had ever happened as dramatically as that night during the flood.

Even after Wes's full recovery and the opportunity to unwind on a Fijian surfing safari, the close call seemed to set Steve back emotionally. The devastation of losing his mother and then nearly losing his best friend weighed heavily on his mind. Steve was not worried about his own mortality and was always very open about it. But the recent events only gave him more cause to think about life and death.

"I can't even think of anything happening to you or Bindi," Steve told me. "I just wouldn't cope."

Seeing Wes lying in a hospital bed made Steve so emotional. It never ceased to amaze me how tough Steve was on the outside, but how deeply loving he was on the inside. He showed his feelings more than any man I ever met. Years after he lost his dog Chilli to a shooting accident (a local man accidentally killed her while he was hunting pigs), he still mourned.

During our nighttime conversations, we spoke at great length about spirituality and belief. Steve's faith had been tremendously tested. At times he would lash out and blame God, and sometimes he would proclaim that he did not believe in God at all. I knew he was just lashing out, and I'd try to use humor to get him back on track.

"You can't have it both ways," I would gently remind him.

When bad things happened to good people, or when innocent animals experienced human cruelty, it shook Steve to the core. His strong feelings demanded deep spiritual answers, and he searched for them all his life.

Hearing the footsteps of his mortality made Steve all the more focused on family. We had a beautiful daughter. Now we wanted a boy.

"One of each would be perfect," Steve said. Seeing the way he played with Bindi made me eager to have another child. Bindi and Steve played together endlessly. Steve was like a big kid himself and could always be counted on for stacks of fun.

I had read about how, through nutrition management, it was possible to sway the odds for having either a boy or a girl. I ducked down to Melbourne to meet with a nutritionist. She gave me all the information for "the boy-baby diet."

I had to cut out dairy, which meant no milk, cheese, yogurt, cottage cheese, or cream cheese. In fact, it was best to cut out calcium altogether. Also, I couldn't have nuts, shellfish, or, alas, chocolate. That was the tough one. Maybe having two girls wouldn't be bad after all.

For his part in our effort to skew our chances toward having a boy, Steve had to keep his nether regions as cool as possible. He was gung ho.

"I'm going to wear an onion bag instead of underpants, babe," he said. "Everything is going to stay real well ventilated." But it was true that keeping his bits cool was an important part of the process, so he made the sacrifice and did his best.

Always, during both the low points and high points in our lives, if we needed to escape, we went bush. We were so lucky to share a passion for wildlife experiences. Tasmania, the beautiful island state off the southern coast of Australia, became one of our favorite wildlife hot spots.

We so loved Tassie's unique wildlife and spectacular wilderness areas that we resolved to establish a conservation property there. Wes and Steve scouted the whole island (in between checking out the top secret Tasmanian surf spots), looking for just the right land for us to purchase.

Part of our motivation was that we did not want to see the Tasmanian devil go the way of the thylacine, the extinct Tasmanian tiger. A bizarre-looking animal, it was shaped like a large dog, with a tail and a pouch like a kangaroo. It had been pushed off of the Australian mainland (probably by the dingo) thousands of years ago, but it was still surviving in Tasmania into the 1930s.

There exists some heartbreaking black-and-white film footage of the only remaining known Tassie tiger in 1936, as the last of the thylacines paces its enclosure. Watching the film is enough to make you rededicate your life to saving wildlife.

With the Tassie tiger gone, its relative, the

Tasmanian devil, became the largest carnivorous marsupial on earth. Any land we would purchase on this island state would have to include a critically important devil habitat. We wanted to make sure they would be with us for centuries to come.

Devils can be quite comical little animals, intense and wild. The Looney Tunes cartoon character "Taz" is an exaggeration, of course, because devils only spin like Taz if they're kept too confined. At the zoo, our devils patrol the boundaries of their enclosures, just as they do their territories in the wild, constantly checking on their turf and guarding it from potential intruders.

The devil got its name from the sound it makes. When they become aggressive over food, devils become extremely vocal, screeching, snarling, growling, and hissing, making the most terrifying noises in the middle of the night over a carcass.

Devils are under threat from a type of cancer called devil facial tumor disease (DFTD). It's a shocking condition where the animal looks as though it's been hit in the face by a shotgun. Huge tumors erupt around its jaws, and the affected animal eventually starves to death.

DFTD is one of only two known contagious cancers in the world, and at this point it is contagious only among devils. The disease was escalating to the point where in some areas of Tasmania, nearly 100 percent of the devil population was gone.

Steve was gravely concerned about the future of the Tassie devils. He was determined to help preserve the species by keeping a healthy population at Australia Zoo. This Noah's ark approach would ensure that the devils didn't go the way of the Tassie tiger.

Amid all the work we did, Steve always managed to fit in some surfing whenever we were in Tasmania. One spot was particularly memorable, since Steve said that it was the best surf of his life. While Bindi and I watched from the beach, Steve could paddle out from the rocks and catch a right-hander that wrapped around the point for about half a mile. Instead of paddling all the way back out, he could hop out, join us for a cuppa, and walk back to the rocks for the next ride. Too easy!

That winter we rented a cabin that we liked, built a big fire in the fireplace, and Steve told stories to Bindi in the evening.

No TV, no video games, just the three of us together, with clean air and good surf. In the morning, we were up before dawn. Bindi and I scraped the ice off the windscreen while Steve packed up his boards, and we headed out.

At the beach, we encountered only a few surfers. The surf in Tasmania can be excellent, but the water is bitterly cold. Steve enjoyed the fact that there were never big crowds, and the locals who braved the water were always lovely people. We would all share lunch and some great stories.

I was an avid reader of *Surf Life* magazine, and I was surprised to discover a write-up of our Tasmanian visit. It made me proud to read how impressed those guys were with Steve's surfing abilities. One incident that didn't make the article was when Steve came partway to shore while I watched him from the beach. All of a sudden he stripped off his wet suit. It was winter and quite cold.

"What are you doing?" I called out.

He stood in the icy water. "This is how dedicated I am to having a boy baby," he said, with a mischievous grin.

I said, "I think you're just supposed to

keep them cool, not actually freeze them off."

He laughed. But I knew this was Steve's way of encouraging me to stick to the boy-baby diet. Did I mention that I could not eat chocolate? The sacrifices we make for love.

Our ongoing Hollywood education included the lesson that moviemaking is not finished once you actually make the movie. After that, you have to promote the movie, because if the audience doesn't show up, all your hard work is a bit pointless.

But before we could sell *Crocodile Hunter: Collision Course* to audiences, we had to sell it to the theater owners who were going to show it to the public. So the first stop for our promotional efforts was a gathering of movie theater exhibitors called Show West, in Las Vegas. We would team up there with Bruce Willis, who had an interest in producing our movie.

Bindi and I had been in Oregon for a few days, visiting family, and we planned to catch up with Steve in Las Vegas. But she and I had an ugly incident at the airport when we arrived. A Vegas lowlife approached us, his hat pulled down, big sunglasses on his face, and displaying some of the worst dentistry I've ever seen.

He leered at us, obviously drunk or crazy, and tried to kiss me. I backed off rapidly and looked for Steve. I knew I could rely on him to take care of any creep I encountered.

Then it dawned on me: The creep *was* Steve. In order to move around the airport without anyone recognizing him, he put on false teeth and changed his usual clothes. I didn't recognize my own husband out of his khakis.

I burst out laughing. Bindi was wide-eyed. "Look, it's your daddy." It took her a while before she was sure.

Our Show West presentation featured live wildlife, organized wonderfully by Wes. Bruce Willis spoke. "I sometimes play an action hero myself," he said, "but you'll see that Steve is a real-life action hero."

Bindi brought a ball python out on stage. Backstage, she and Bruce hit it off. He has three daughters of his own, and he immediately connected with Bindi. They wound up playing with the lion cubs and the other animals that Wes had organized there.

We embarked on a twelve-city North American promotion tour, and then hit London, Dublin, and Glasgow. To buzz us around, MGM provided the corporate jet, with a crocodile painted on the side. It was a whirlwind tour. Bindi would get into a limousine in one city, we would carry her sleeping onto the plane, and then she would wake up in a limousine in a different city. It was nonstop.

My sister Bonnie came with us to care for Bindi while Steve and I did interviews, one after another, from the morning shows to late-night television. We spoke as well with reporters from newspapers, magazines, and radio programs. Over the course of six weeks, we did twelve hundred interviews.

Our publicist, Andrew Bernstein, gave Steve one of his favorite compliments. "I've never seen anybody promote a movie harder," he said, "except maybe Tom Cruise."

Steve and Andrew hit it off quite well, but Steve was concerned that Andrew was single and didn't have a girlfriend. "Come out with me," Steve said to Andrew one evening on the plane. "We can go clubbing, and I'll make sure you have a great time."

Steve added with a laugh, "You know, Andrew, for some reason chicks really dig me. I don't know why, since I'm such a big ugly bloke, but they will come up and talk to me. Mate, I can pull you chicks, no problem at all."

"Steve," Andrew said as gently as he could, "I like women, but I don't *like* women."

"Oh, don't worry about it," Steve blustered on, still not getting it. "We'll have a great time."

Andrew got up to use the restroom on the plane. I leaned over to Steve. "Andrew is trying to tell you that he's gay," I said.

Steve's eyes got really big. As soon as Andrew stepped out of the restroom, Steve piped up. "Andrew, don't worry about it, blokes love me. We'll go out and I'll get you blokes."

I just about died from embarrassment. But Andrew laughed, and then we all started laughing. Andrew and Steve ended up becoming fast friends.

Once again, Wes organized animals for the Los Angeles premiere of *Crocodile Hunter*. We had a red carpet like no other. Steve, Bindi, and I came down it on an elephant. Wes brought in a giraffe, cheetahs, and an alligator. Steve climbed up on the elephant alone, and the trainer had her rear straight up in the air. The pictures were priceless.

All our promotional work paid off. *Crocodile Hunter: Collision Course* grossed more in the first weekend than the cost of filming. The movie promotion had been a hard slog, so after we got back home we planned a more leisurely getaway to Singapore and the Maldive Islands.

Steve loved the Singapore Zoo and always considered it a sister zoo to our own. Bindi and I enjoyed being in Singapore with Steve, because he had spent so much time in Southeast Asia and really knew his way around.

Every morning Steve would head out into the streets of Singapore and discover a new and yummy local curry for breakfast. Bindi watched her daddy carefully. She would eat her mild curry while Steve ate his spicy one. She followed along with everything that he did.

One morning at the hotel, Bindi came out in her pajamas while I was trying to get her dressed. She was halfway there and was prancing around in her little pajama top, with no bottoms.

Suddenly she spotted the tea set in the room and decided to make tea. I helped her out. She made green tea for all of us, carefully poured it, and took it over to Steve with a big smile, bare bottom and all.

"When was the last time you had a girl with no underpants fix you tea?" I asked Steve, laughing.

Without missing a beat, Steve said, "The last time I was in Singapore."

"You're a dag," I said, knowing that the last time Steve was in Singapore was before we were married. Bindi didn't get the joke, but Steve and I laughed and laughed.

We hit the Maldives for a surfing break. The islands are right on the equator, and the heat was incredible. Bindi didn't understand traditional Muslim clothing. The women wore black burkas, with just a small panel to look through, and Bindi worried about them in the heat. Somewhere along the line, she had picked up some verbiage that she then blurted out loudly in the street when we encountered a heavily swathed Muslim woman.

"Mummy, is that an oppressed woman?" Not wanting to cause an incident, I hustled us both away. I tried to explain about differences in cultures and religions, how sometimes what you wore was an indication of modesty, rather than oppression. But in the back of my mind was the thought, *Out of the mouths of babes.*

Even on the road, we continued our efforts to conceive. Part of our boy-baby effort was the need to try right at the time of ovulation. I packed an ovulation kit with me everywhere. When the strip turned blue, it meant we had a twenty-four- to forty-eight-hour window to get busy.

At first I had Steve convinced that women ovulated twenty or thirty times a month. But I couldn't trick him forever. At some point he realized that that was impossible.

Upon returning to Australia, we headed out to the Brigalow Belt, an endangered bush habitat that stretches from New South Wales north into Queensland. It's named after a wattle, or tree, species, but because of intense land clearing, the whole region was in trouble.

We had purchased eighty thousand acres to help protect this fragile environment. Steve wanted to check up on our dams, which had been built a hundred or more years ago. These dams had never before dried out. Now we were battling a severe drought that the land hadn't seen in ages. Decades worth of silt had built up in the dams and was fifteen feet deep in places.

While there was still water in the middle of the pools, animals attempted to reach it through the silt but would get bogged. We spent day after day checking dams, finding about eight to ten animals hopelessly mired in the silt at each and every dam, primarily kangaroos and wallabies.

We had to get to the dams early in the morning. Some of the kangaroos had been struggling all night. Steve engineered planks and straps to rescue the animals. The silt would suck us down just as fast, so we had to be careful going out to rescue the roos. Because of the lactic acid buildup in their tissues (a product of their all-night exertions to free themselves), some of the kangaroos were too far gone and couldn't recover. But we saved quite a few.

At one point, Bob came out to lend a hand. I was at the homestead, and the ovulation strip turned bright blue. I hustled over to the creek bed where Steve and his dad were working.

I motioned to Steve. "The strip is blue," I said. He looked around nervously.

"I'm out here working with me dad," he said. "What do you want me to do?"

"Just come on," I whispered impatiently.

"But my dad's right here!"

I smiled and took his hand. We headed up the dry creek bed and spent some quality time with the biting ants and the prickles.

It was after this trip to our conservation property in the Brigalow Belt that I discovered I was pregnant. I tried to let Steve know by sitting down at the table and tucking into a bowl of ice cream and pickles.

"What are you doing?" asked a totally confused Steve. I explained, and we were both totally overjoyed, keeping our fingers crossed for a boy to go along with our darling daughter.

With the news that he would soon be a daddy again, Steve seemed inspired to work even harder. Our zoo continued to get busier, and we had trouble coping with the large numbers. The biggest draw was the crocodiles. Crowds poured in for the croc shows, filling up all the grandstands. The place was packed.

Steve came up with a monumental plan.

He was a big fan of the Colosseum-type arenas of the Roman gladiator days. He sketched out his idea for me on a piece of paper.

"Have a go at this, it's a coliseum," he declared, his eyes wide with excitement. He drew an oval, then a series of smaller ovals in back of it. "Then we have crocodile ponds where the crocs could live. Every day a different croc could come out for the show and swim through a canal system"—he sketched rapidly—"then come out in the main area."

"Canals," I said. "Could you get them to come in on cue?"

"Piece of cake!" he said. "And get this! We call it . . . the Crocoseum!"

His enthusiasm was contagious. Never mind that nothing like this had ever been done before. Steve was determined to take the excitement and hype of the ancient Roman gladiators and combine it with the need to show people just how awesome crocs really were.

But it was a huge project. There was nothing to compare it to, because nothing even remotely similar had ever been attempted anywhere in the world. I priced it out: The budget to build the arena would have to be somewhere north of eight million dollars, a huge expense. Wes, John, Frank, and I all knew we'd have to rely on Steve's knowledge of crocodiles to make this work.

Steve's enthusiasm never waned. He was determined. This would become the biggest structure at the zoo. The arena would seat five thousand and have space beneath it for museums, shops, and a food court. The center of the arena would have land areas large enough for people to work around crocodiles safely and water areas large enough for crocs to be able to access them easily.

"How is this going to work, Steve?" I asked, after soberly assessing the cost. What if we laid out more than eight million dollars and the crocodiles decided not to cooperate? "How are you going to convince a crocodile to come out exactly at show-time, try to kill and eat the keeper, and then go back home again?"

I bit my tongue when I realized what was coming out of my mouth: advice on crocodiles directed at the world's expert on croc behavior. Steve was right with his philosophy: *Build it, and they will come.*

These were heady times. As the Crocoseum rose into the sky, my tummy got bigger and bigger with our new baby. It felt like I was expanding as rapidly as the new project.

The Crocoseum debuted during an Animal Planet live feed, its premiere beamed all over the world. The design was a smashing success. Once again, Steve had confounded the doubters.

We decided we didn't really want to know if we were having a boy or a girl. "Why would you want to know?" I said. "The amount of work you go through in labor—at least you have something to work toward, a big surprise, the payoff at the end."

"Oh, I never found labor difficult at all," Steve said with a grin. "Sometimes it was painful when you would squeeze my hand a bit hard, but other than that . . ."

He never got a chance to finish. I attacked him. He rolled around the floor, laughing.

At one point, we were in the kitchen talking when, out of the blue, Steve changed the subject. "If we have another little girl," Steve asked, "would you go again?"

"Absolutely," I said, without hesitation.

"Bindi is the joy of our lives. I'm sure this little baby will be the same. Boy or girl, I'd go again."

It was a Sunday at the end of November, which meant summertime in Australia. My water broke at night, and this time I knew what was coming. I remember thinking, *There's no turning back now.* Immediately after my water broke, the contractions started. I had been sleeping in Bindi's room because I was so awkward and uncomfortable that I kept waking everybody up. Plus, Bindi loved being able to snuggle down in bed with her daddy.

I crept into their room quietly. As I stood beside the bed, I leaned in next to Steve's ear. I could feel his breath. He smelled warm and sweet and familiar. *He is going to be a daddy again,* I thought, *his favorite job in the world.*

When I whispered "Steve," he opened his eyes without moving. Bindi slept on at his side. It was about midnight, and I told Steve that we didn't have to leave for the hospital yet, but it would be soon. Once he was satisfied that I was okay, I headed back to Bindi's bed to get some rest.

Throughout our life together, I never knew

what Steve was going to say next. True to form, he came to my bedside, not long after I lay down, and said, "I'm putting my foot down."

"What?"

"The baby is going to be named Robert Clarence Irwin if it's a boy," he said. Robert after his dad, Bob, and Clarence after my dad.

"You don't need to put your foot down," I whispered to him. "I think it's a beautiful name."

When my contractions were four minutes apart, I knew it was time to head to the hospital. It was five o'clock in the morning. Steve got everything organized to take me. Of course, one of the things he grabbed was a camera. He was determined that we would capture everything on film. We called Trevor, our friend and cinematographer who had filmed Bindi's birth, to meet us at the hospital, and Thelma, Bindi's nanny, came over to get her off to school.

As we drove in the car, Steve filmed me from the driver's seat. As he shot, the Ute slowly edged toward the side of the road. He looked up, grabbed the wheel, and corrected the steering. Then he went back to filming and the whole thing happened again. After two or three veers, I had had enough.

"Stop filming," I yelled. He quickly put the camera down. I think he realized that this was no time to argue with mama bear.

At the hospital, an attendant brought down a wheelchair for me. Steve somehow managed, without a forklift, to get me out of the truck and into the wheelchair. The birth progressed a lot faster than it had with Bindi. I wasn't worried because I had Steve with me, and I knew everything would be fine, as long as we were together.

I pushed like an Olympic baby pusher. I should have gotten the gold for my pushing. I think I pushed until I was nearly inside out.

The baby came. Steve said, "It's a boy!" and brought him to me. I remember my son's tiny pink mouth. He looked like a baby bird with his eyes closed and his mouth open. He immediately began feeding. Steve cried tears of joy.

Once we got settled, the proud papa headed for Sunshine Coast Grammar School to tell Bindi the news. "You've got a little brother," he told her. Bindi was elated, in spite of the fact that she had spent every night saying her prayers for a little sister. Steve brought her to the hospital, where she took her little brother in her arms and looked at him lovingly.

"How do you know he's a boy?" she asked.

"Bindi," Thelma said, "they're not born with clothes on."

"I think I will name him Brian," Bindi said.

"His name is Robert," Steve told her.

"Oh, well," Bindi said. "I'm going to call him Brian for short."

It was a Sunday, December 1, 2003, and we had all just received the best Christmas present ever. Robert Clarence Irwin. Baby Bob.

Steve loved showing off his new son. When we brought him home, all the zoo staff welcomed the new arrival.

We have always had a good relationship with a group of Buddhist monks from Tibet. They had blessed Bindi when she was a newborn. As Robert celebrated his one-month birthday, we decided to hold a fund-raiser for a Buddhist nun's convent where the well had dried up.

A new well would cost forty thousand

dollars. We felt that amount might be achievable in a series of fund-raising events. We invited the nuns to stay at Australia Zoo and planned to hold a fund-raiser at our brand-new Crocoseum, doing our part to help raise some money for the new well.

The nuns wished to know if we wanted them to bless the animals while they were at the zoo. "Would you please bless Robert?" we asked.

Bindi had been blessed along with the crocodiles when she was a month old. Now we would do the same for Robert. The nuns came into the Crocoseum for the ceremony. I brought a sleepy little Robert, adorned with his prayer flag and a scarf. We invited press to help publicize the plight of the nuns. Robert was very peaceful. The nuns sang, chanted, and gave him their special blessing.

The ceremony was over, and the croc show was about to begin. Steve wanted to share Robert's first crocodile show with everyone at the Crocoseum, as he was going to feed Murray the crocodile.

Just as we had done with Bindi at this age, we brought Robert out for the show.

Steve talked to the visitors about how proud he was of his son. He pointed out the crocodile to Baby Bob. Although Robert had been in with the crocodiles before, and would be again, this was an event where we could share the moment with everybody.

When the croc show was over, Steve brought Robert back underneath the Crocoseum and I put him in his stroller. His eyes were big and he was waving his arms. This event would mark the beginning of a lifetime of working with his father as a wildlife warrior. Steve and Bindi were regulars during the croc shows, and now it looked as though Robert would be joining in as well.

Later that day, a message was forwarded to us. One of the television channels covering the event at the Crocoseum had decided to put a negative slant on the story.

“How crazy could that be?” I said to Steve. “What negative aspect could you possibly find in such a beautiful event?”

Having children growing up at a zoo prompted some people to feel that ours was somehow not a suitable lifestyle. We had occasionally encountered this opinion before and always managed simply to agree to disagree with the naysayers. So we weren't worried.

We finished our day. Steve cooked dinner. I hung freshly laundered clothes on the line. Robert slept in his stroller. Bindi was outside, running around visiting with her fairy friends in the bushes.

Then the news broke. And it broke like a tidal wave. It wasn't just one television station that had picked up the story. There appeared to be a collective decision to crucify Steve for having Robert at the crocodile show with him.

Everything stopped. Dinner stopped. We stopped. The phone calls started.

The story had gone out all over the world. Steve was portrayed as an evil, ugly monster who had exploited his son in some kind of stunt show. It is difficult to grasp the atmosphere at the center of a media attack unless it has happened to you. I felt as though the mob was going to be outside our gates with lighted torches.

Part of the problem was the infamous Michael Jackson "baby-dangling" incident, which had occurred just over a year before: The pop star hung his baby out a hotel window in Berlin to adoring fans waiting below.

The press played the two stories off each other. Steve and Michael, a couple of baby danglers.

We didn't know what to do. It was as though we were being hunted. Steve went off to the back block of the zoo to try to get his head around everything that had been happening. He built a fire and gazed into it.

I didn't have to think about it. I knew beyond certainty that the most important part of Steve's life was his family. His children meant everything to him. All of a sudden, my wonderful, sharing, protective husband was being condemned. His crime was sharing wildlife experiences with Robert, exactly as he had done for the last five and a half years with Bindi.

The media circus escalated. Helicopters hovered over the zoo, trying to snag any glimpse of the crazy Irwin family. Steve erected shade cloth around our yard for privacy. We soon realized we couldn't go anywhere. There would be no visits to the zoo, no answering the phone, no doing croc shows. The criticism and the spin continued.

I stood by Steve's side and watched his heart break. I couldn't believe the mean-spirited, petty, awful people in the world. Editors manipulated film footage, trying to make the croc look bigger or closer to Robert than it actually was. What possible end could that serve?

I have seen Tasmanian devils battle over a carcass. I have seen lionesses crowding a kill, dingoes on the trail of a feral piglet, an adult croc thrashing its prey to pieces. But never, in all the animal world, have I witnessed anything to match the casual cruelty of the human being.

It was about to get worse. We stepped off a very dark cliff indeed.

CHAPTER SIXTEEN

Antarctica

The same night the Baby Bob controversy hit, we were still reeling with the unexpected fallout when a police officer stopped by. The governor-general, the officer said, required Steve to contact him immediately.

"I'm not sure exactly where Steve is," I said. I only knew that he was somewhere in the back block, contemplating the day's events.

"It would be good if Steve could make that call tonight," the officer said.

When Steve came in and called the number the police gave, the governor-general's secretary answered. She was quite terse and to the point. She indicated that we would be investigated by Children's Services.

"I don't understand why you are calling me at ten o'clock on a Friday night to tell me that," Steve said. I could hear the sharp edge in the woman's voice even though Steve held the phone.

"Be very careful, Mr. Irwin," she said. "We have the capacity to take your children."

I will never forget what that woman said or the way in which she said it. Could the social workers come and take our children away? Children who were so desperately loved, taken care of, and cherished?

This was a media beat-up at its very worst. All those officials reacting to what the media labeled "The Baby Bob Incident" failed to understand the Irwin family. This is what we did—teach our children about wildlife, from a very early age. It wasn't unnatural and it wasn't a stunt. It was, on the contrary, an old and valued family tradition, and one that I embraced wholeheartedly.

It was who we were. To have the press fasten on the practice as irresponsible made us feel that our very ability as parents was being attacked. It didn't make any sense.

This is why Steve never publicly apologized. For him to say "I'm sorry" would mean that he was sorry that Bob and Lyn raised him the way they did, and that was simply impossible. The best he could do was to sincerely apologize if he had worried anyone. The reality was that he would have been remiss as a parent if he didn't teach his kids how to coexist with wildlife. After all, his kids didn't just have busy roads and hot stoves to contend with. They literally had to learn how to live with crocodiles and venomous snakes in their backyard.

Through it all, the plight of the Tibetan nuns was completely and totally ignored. The world media had not a word to spare about a dry well that hundreds of people depended on. For months, any time Steve encountered the press, Tibetan nuns were about the furthest thing from the reporter's mind. The questions would always be the same: "Hey, Stevo, what about the Baby Bob Incident?"

"If I could relive Friday, mate, I'd go surfing," Steve said on a hugely publicized national television appearance in the United States. "I can't go back to Friday, but you know what, mate? Don't think for one second I would ever endanger my children, mate, because they're the most important thing in my life, just like I was with my mum and dad."

Steve and I struggled to get back to a point where we felt normal again. Sponsors spoke about terminating contracts. Members of our own documentary crew sought to distance themselves from us, and our relationship with Discovery was on shaky ground.

But gradually we were able to tune out the static and hear what people were saying. Not the press, but the people. We read the e-mails that had been pouring in, as well as faxes, letters, and phone messages. Real people helped to get us back on track. Their kids were growing up with them on cattle ranches and could already drive tractors, or lived on horse farms and helped handle skittish stallions. Other children were learning to be gymnasts, a sport which was physically rigorous and held out the chance of injury. The parents had sent us messages of support.

"Don't feel bad, Steve," wrote one eleven-year-old from Sydney. "It's not the wildlife that's dangerous." A mother wrote us, "I have a new little baby, and if you want to take him in on the croc show it is okay with me."

So many parents employed the same phrase: "I'd trust my kids with Steve any day."

I knew Steve was starting to cope when he proposed one of his most ambitious documentaries with John. They would journey literally to the end of the earth, to Antarctica, and document conditions for wildlife there. Steve knew that Antarctica functioned as a canary in a coal mine—an early-warning mechanism for environmental problems with the earth as a whole.

It was summer in the Southern Hemisphere, and that's the only practical time to go to Antarctica, but the continent was still no place for small children. I felt torn about being separated at such a tumultuous time, but the doco *Icebreaker* had been planned for a long time. Steve went south with John Stainton and a camera crew. I went to Florida and Disney World with the rest of my family: Robert and Bindi.

As he had with the fauna of the Galapagos Islands, Steve discovered that the Antarctic wildlife had little fear of humans.

There were no hunting parties out terrorizing the wildlife, so they didn't perceive people as a threat. The penguins were among the friendliest. In fact, he found if he mimicked their actions, they would often repeat them in response. Steve slid on his belly down the slopes of ice, and the penguins did the same.

He maintained a respectful distance, but often the penguins came to him. Steve was really interested in learning more about penguins' main predator, leopard seals. The seals had a fierce reputation. One report detailed the recent fatal encounter of a researcher from New Zealand with a leopard seal. But after visiting Antarctica, Steve came away with a different perception.

It turned out that the researcher was snorkeling at the time, and the seal actually seemed to be playing with her. The leopard seal grabbed her flipper and pulled her under the water. Then it let her go, and she swam to the surface. But the seal pulled her down again and again, like it was a game. Finally she was unable to hold her breath long enough.

The facts didn't make the event any less tragic, but it did put a new perspective on human interaction with leopard seals. Steve watched the leopard seals emerge from the holes in the ice.

"They are like great big caterpillars," he told me. As with crocs, they could be dangerous in the water, or lunging out from the water's edge. But once the seals were out of the water, they resembled gigantic inchworms coming at you. They were really no threat as far as chasing a human down.

The best approach to a leopard seal was to give it a wide berth. Steve was able to talk about leopard seal behavior while sitting on the ice with one nearby. The seal didn't fling itself at Steve. In fact, it listened as Steve told its story, then slipped back into the water.

Antarctica had definite rules about approaching wildlife. Penguins, for example, had a specific distance restriction, meaning all humans had to stay at least that distance away—unless the penguin approached them. That was the rule.

The reality was a little different. Researchers had to proceed through great numbers of the birds just to walk to the dunny. Tourist boats, which came to Antarctica in large numbers, plowed through penguins when approaching ports, actually killing them in droves.

Steve felt determined to focus on the positive aspects of his experience. Humpback whales came up to the side of the boat, lifting their huge heads out of the water, having a look around. There was no need to go searching for them—the natural curiosity of the humpbacks made them come to you. Steve donned his dry suit to do some filming in the water. The whales approached. Because Steve's dry suit had a small leak in it, he climbed up on a growler—a small iceberg—and was able to hang on to complete the filming.

The resulting footage represented what Steve was all about. He was able to bring his experience with these beautiful whales into people's living rooms. This is why he did what he did—to get wildlife into our hearts.

The waters of Antarctica are officially deemed protected by international treaty. Every year, however, Japanese fleets come in to conduct "research" on whales, under the auspices of JARPA (Japanese Whale Research Program in Antarctica). It's curious research: The boatmen kill whales, take the meat back to Japan, and put it on the market. No viable research information on whales ever results.

The Japanese government seems to have made whale killing a point of national pride. The traffic in whale meat is not even a lucrative business, only about forty million dollars a year worldwide. In fact, most Japanese people are against whaling and would rather not even eat whale meat. But the killing continues, even though the Japanese are no longer dependent on whales for food, as they were during World War II.

As a wildlife warrior, Steve fought against age-old practices that were destroying entire species. He felt it was time to focus on the nonconsumptive use of wildlife. Poachers were still hunting tigers for their bones, and bears for their gallbladders, all for traditional medicines that have been far surpassed by modern pharmaceuticals.

It should be simple. We should be able to take an aspirin instead of powdered rhino horn, make whaling something that we read about in history books, and end our appetite for shark-fin soup, which is causing one of the world's most ancient and important species to vanish from the oceans.

Until the day comes when the senseless killing ends, we will all have to fight like wildlife warriors to protect our precious planet.

Steve came back from his Antarctica trip with renewed determination. In his last documentary, Steve showed how penguins actually play. He tried to demystify the fierce reputation of the leopard seal. He talked about how humpback whales have a family structure similar to ours, that they are mammals, they love their children, and they communicate.

But in the wake of the Baby Bob incident, reporters seemed to be lying in wait for Steve. This time he was attacked for filming with the wildlife of Antarctica. Commentators characterized Steve sliding down the slippery slopes with penguins as "interfering." Sitting near a leopard seal to demonstrate that they aren't horrible monsters was labeled as "displacing wildlife." Most ludicrous of all, when Steve sat on the growler, a report claimed he was riding a whale.

Australian authorities launched an official investigation. Laws regulated procedures of filming Antarctic wildlife, and the charges, if proven, included potential jail time. Just months after being devastated by claims that he wasn't a good father, Steve faced charges that he was a wildlife harasser, instead of a wildlife warrior. We found ourselves spending money on lawyers that should have been going to wildlife conservation.

The controversy highlighted the way wildlife is prioritized. Steve and I believed that in the modern age, wildlife competes for headlines with politics and sports. Watching wildlife on the long lens ("See that little dot on the center of that iceberg?") just won't work anymore. It won't put wildlife into people's hearts or give them a priority in the press, which is where they have to be to have any chance of survival.

Steve had such genuine love for wildlife and was so skilled and gifted, he was able to share the animals' beauty without using restraining devices. For example, whales spend a tenth of their lives at the surface of the ocean. Whale watching doesn't harm whales. But it is highly effective in getting people to take whales into their hearts.

More than that, Steve wanted everyone

watching to feel like they were sharing the experience and not just viewing it. "I want you in there with me, mate," Steve told his audiences. "I'm taking you right in there with me." He wanted everyone to come with him on his journey of discovery and to connect with wildlife as he did.

In the end, the investigation determined that Steve had done nothing wrong on the Antarctic documentary trip. Once again, the thoughts and prayers of ordinary people around the world who believed in Steve sustained us. I wouldn't have blamed him if he had thrown it all in. "I'm closing the gates," he could have said. "I'm going to quit struggling." But he wasn't willing to give up or give in.

Steve kept fighting, but not since he'd lost his mother had I seen him so low. He had taken two hits in quick succession: first Baby Bob, then the Antarctica allegations.

"Crocodiles are easy," Steve said. "They try to kill and eat you. People are harder. Sometimes they pretend to be your friend first."

Steve was a warrior in every sense of the word, but battling wildlife perpetrators just wasn't the same as old-fashioned combat. Because Steve's knees continued to deteriorate, his surfing ability was severely compromised. Instead of giving up in despair, Steve sought another outlet for all his pent-up energy.

Through our head of security, Dan Higgins, Steve discovered mixed martial arts (or MMA) fighting. Steve was a natural at sparring. His build was unbelievable, like a gorilla's, with his thick chest, long arms, and outrageous strength for hugging things (like crocs). Once he grabbed hold of something, there was no getting away. He had a punch equivalent to the kick of a Clydesdale, he could just about lift somebody off the ground with an uppercut, and he took to grappling as a wonderful release. Steve never did anything by halves.

I remember one time the guys were telling him that a good body shot could really wind someone. Steve suddenly said, "No one's given me a good body shot. Try to drop me with a good one so I know what it feels like." Steve opened up his arms and Dan just pile drove him. Steve said, in between gasps, "Thanks, mate. That was great, I get your point."

I would join in and spar or work the pads, or roll around until I was absolutely exhausted. Steve would go until he threw up. I've never seen anything like it. Some MMA athletes are able to seek that dark place, that point of total exhaustion—they can see it, stare at it, and sometimes get past it. Steve ran to it every day. He wasn't afraid of it. He tried to get himself to that point of exhaustion so that maybe the next day he could get a little bit further.

Soon we were recruiting the crew, anyone who had any experience grappling. Guys from the tiger department or construction were lining up to have a go, and Steve would go through the blokes one after another, grappling away. And all the while I loved it too.

Here was something else that Steve and I could do together, and he was hilarious. Sometimes he would be cooking dinner, and I'd come into the kitchen and pat him on the bum with a flirtatious look. The next thing I knew he had me in underhooks and I was on the floor. We'd be rolling around, laughing, trying to grapple each other. It's like the old adage when you're watching a wildlife documentary: Are they fighting or mating?

It seems odd that this no-holds-barred fighting really brought us closer, but we had so much fun with it. Steve finally built his own dojo on a raised concrete pad with a cage, shade cloth, fans, mats, bags, and all that great gear. Six days a week, he would start grappling at daylight, as soon as the guys would get into work. He had his own set of techniques and was a great brawler in his own right, having stood up for himself in some of the roughest, toughest, most remote outback areas.

Steve wasn't intimidated by anyone. Dan Higgins brought a bunch of guys over from the States, including Keith Jardine and other pros, and Steve couldn't wait to tear into them. He held his own against some of the best MMA fighters in the world. I always thought that if he'd wanted to be a fighter as a profession, he would have been dangerous. All the guys heartily agreed.

Steve was off for another trip—this time, he was headed for Washington, D.C., to address the Discovery Channel's four-thousand-person staff as part of the cable giant's twenty-year birthday party. He was happy to go over, since it was a big deal for Discovery and Steve was very proud to be asked to speak to their team. But it was difficult for him to be away.

It seemed that now, more than ever, he relished having his little family unit. Now that Robert was getting bigger, Steve was enjoying spending time with both the kids and seemed much more appreciative of how comfortable our relationship had become. I was pleasantly surprised when the phone rang and it was Steve, calling all the way from Washington, D.C.

He sounded concerned. "Mate, when I hugged you good-bye at the airport, it felt like there was something wrong."

I was always impressed with the way Steve could tune in to my feelings. "The longer we're together, the more I worry when we're apart," I confessed.

"We just have to make every day, every minute we're together count," Steve replied.

"I know," I told him. "I just miss you so much."

"Don't worry, babe," he said. "I'll be home in a couple days. Big cities just aren't my cup of tea."

When he did come home, we had new Sumatran tiger cubs to play with at the zoo, and new bush adventures to embark upon. Professor Craig Franklin of the University of Queensland mounted a crocodile research partnership with Steve. The idea was to fasten transmitters and data loggers on crocs to record their activity in their natural environment. But in order to place the transmitters, you had to catch the crocs first, and that's where Steve's expertise came in.

Steve never felt more content than when he was with his family in the bush. "There's nothing more valuable than human life, and this research will help protect both crocs and people," he told us. The bush was where Steve felt most at home. It was where he was at his best. On that one trip, he caught thirty-three crocs in fourteen days.

He wanted to do more. "I'd really like to have the capability of doing research on the ocean as well as in the rivers," he told me. "I could do so much more for crocodiles and sharks if I had a purpose-built research vessel."

I could see where he was heading. I was not a big fan of boats.

"I'm going to contact a company in Western Australia, in Perth," he said. "I'm going to work on a custom-built research vessel."

As the wheels turned in his mind, he became more and more excited. "The sky's the limit, mate," he said. "We could help tiger sharks and learn why crocs go out to sea. There is no reason why we couldn't help whales, too."

"Tell me how we can help whales," I said, expecting to hear about a research project that he and Craig had in mind.

"It will be great," he said. "We'll build a boat with an ice-breaking hull. We'll weld a can opener to the front, and join Sea Shepherd in Antarctica to stop those whaling boats in their tracks."

When we got back from our first trip to Cape York Peninsula with Craig Franklin, Steve immediately began drawing up plans for his boat. He wanted to make it as comfortable as possible. As he envisioned it, the boat would be somewhere between a hardcore scientific research vessel and a luxury cruiser.

He designed three berths, a plasma screen television for the kids, and air-conditioned comfort below deck. He placed a big marlin board off the back, for Jet Skis, shark cages, or hauling out huge crocs. One feature that he was really adamant about was a helicopter pad. He designed the craft so that the helicopter could land on the top. Steve's design plans went back and forth to Perth for months.

"I want this boat's primary function to be crocodile research and rescue work," Steve said. "So I'm going to name her *Croc One*."

"Why don't we call it *For Sale* instead?" I suggested.

I'm not sure Steve saw the humor in that. *Croc One* was his baby. But for some reason, I felt tremendous trepidation about this boat. I attributed my feelings of concern to Bindi and Robert. Anytime you have kids on a boat, the rules change—no playing hide-and-seek, no walking on deck without a life jacket on. It made me uncomfortable to think about being two hundred miles out at sea with two young kids.

We had had so many wild adventures together as a family that, ultimately, I had to trust Steve. But my support for *Croc One* was always, deep down, halfhearted at best. I couldn't shake my feeling of foreboding about it.

Over the course of two years, from June

2004 to June 2006, two separate deaths did nothing to ease my overall anxiety. Steve's beloved Staffordshire bull terrier Sui died of cancer in June 2004. He had set up his swag and slept beside her all night, talking to her, recalling old times in the bush catching crocodiles, and comforting her.

Losing Sui brought up memories of losing Chilli a decade and a half earlier. "I am not getting another dog," Steve said. "It is just too painful."

Wes, the most loyal friend anyone could have, was there for Steve while Sui passed from this life to the next. Wes shared in Steve's grief. They had known Sui longer than Steve and I had been together.

Two years after Sui's death, in June 2006, we lost Harriet. At 175, Harriet was the oldest living creature on earth. She had met Charles Darwin and sailed on the *Beagle*. She was our link to the past at the zoo, and beyond that, our link to the great scientist himself. She was a living museum and an icon of our zoo.

The kids and I were headed to Fraser Island, along the southern coast of Queensland, with Joy, Steve's sister, and her husband, Frank, our zoo manager, when I heard the news. An ultrasound had confirmed that Harriet had suffered a massive heart attack.

Steve called me. "I think you'd better come home."

"I should talk to the kids about this," I said.

Bindi was horrified. "How long is Harriet going to live?" she asked.

"Maybe hours, maybe days, but not long."

"I don't want to see Harriet die," she said resolutely. She wanted to remember her as the healthy, happy tortoise with whom she'd grown up.

From the time Bindi was a tiny baby, she would enter Harriet's enclosure, put her arms around the tortoise's massive shell, and rest her face against her carapace, which was always warm from the sun. Harriet's favorite food was hibiscus flowers, and Bindi would collect them by the dozen to feed her dear friend.

I was worried about Steve but told him that Bindi couldn't bear to see Harriet dying. "It's okay," he said. "Wes is here with me." Once again, it fell to Wes to share his best mate's grief.

One of my favorite memories of Harriet

was when John Edward, the psychic medium, came to the zoo. He found out almost by accident that he could read living animals. Everything Harriet communicated to him was absolutely spot-on.

Although John hadn't been to the zoo before, Harriet told him that she used to be in another enclosure and that she liked this one better. That made sense because her current enclosure was bigger. Harriet also said that she liked the keeper with an accent, but it wasn't Australian or American. John was having trouble placing the accent, and then he met Jan, who was English. "That's the accent," he said. Turns out Jan had been taking care of Harriet since before I had ever visited the zoo. John also said that Harriet had had blood drawn from her tail—which was correct, since we'd done a DNA profile on her.

One thing, though, John had wrong. "Harriet misses her blanket," he said.

"You know, John," I said, "Harriet can't have a blanket, because she tries to eat everything."

"She misses her blanket," John politely insisted.

After he left the zoo, I asked Steve about it. "Did Harriet ever have a blanket?"

Steve laughed. "Nah, mate, she'd have just eaten it."

Weeks went by. I visited Steve's dad, Bob, and told him about everything John Edward had said, right up to the blanket. "He was spot-on until he got to the blanket," I said.

Bob's face widened with a big grin. "Actually, back in the eighties," he said, "a woman knitted a blanket for Harriet. On cold nights, before we had given Harriet a heat lamp, we would put the blanket over her shell, hoping that it would help contain some of her heat during the night."

I laughed. I couldn't believe it. Bob said, "Harriet had that blanket for weeks and weeks, until one day she tried to eat it. Then we had to take it away."

Even in the midst of loss, Steve managed to concentrate on future projects. One included plans to work with Philippe Cousteau Jr., the grandson of one of Steve's heroes, the pioneering oceanographer Jacques Cousteau, on a documentary called *Ocean's Deadliest*.

CHAPTER SEVENTEEN

The School of the Bush

On July 25, 2006—the day after Bindi's eighth birthday celebration, and the dead of winter in mild, sunny Queensland—we headed out for the Cape York Peninsula on a five-week croc research trip.

Once again, we partnered with the University of Queensland's Professor Craig Franklin. Steve's instincts, experience, and scientific curiosity about crocodiles married well with the academic world.

He certainly put his Crocodile Hunter money where his heart was. We spent hundreds of thousands of dollars on the scientific equipment, travel costs, trapping gear, and the infrastructure to support the big research team. For the first time, we would employ time-depth recorders as well as satellite tracking to trace croc behavior.

Although crocodiles have remained virtually unchanged for nearly sixty-five million years, our lack of understanding of their habits is shocking. No one knows much of anything about them. No scientific data exists, for example, on what percentage of crocodiles reach maturity in the wild. Is it one in fifty? One in one hundred? One in two hundred? The last figure seems to be the best guess, but a guess it is.

It seemed the more we studied crocs, the more questions we had. For example, we know that crocs eat fish, as well as mammals that venture too close to the water's edge. But many crocodiles live in salt water, where no mammals would come down for a drink. So what do they eat?

This would be the first croc research trip where both Bindi and Robert were old enough to participate. Robert was two and a half, and walking and talking like a serious little man. Bindi, of course, had been involved in croc research trips before. But now she had new motivation. We were in the middle of filming her own nature show, *Bindi the Jungle Girl*.

This was important for Steve. "There'd be nothing that would make me happier than having Bindi just take over filming and I could take it easy and run the zoo, do my conservation work, and let Bindi have the limelight," Steve would say.

It might have seemed like an unusual thing to say about a kid who just turned eight, but Bindi was no ordinary kid. She had a calling. I would sense it when I was around her, just as I sensed it when I first met Steve.

Although Bindi was a regular kid most of the time—playing and being goofy, with me making her eat her vegetables, brush her teeth, and go to school on time—there were many moments when I'd see someone who'd been here before. Bindi would participate in the filming in such a way that she always made sure a certain conservation message came through, or she'd want to do a take again to make sure her words got the message across properly.

I continued to marvel at the wise being in this little person's body. I kept catching glimpses, like snapshots through the window of a moving train, of this person who knew she was working toward making the world a better place. Watching her evolve was truly special.

And here was our training ground, here was our school of the bush: the Cape York Peninsula, Lakefield National Park, one of our favorite places in the world. Bindi and Robert were familiar with the area from our research trip the year before, and they returned to it like an old friend.

Although Steve never much liked to drive in cities, as soon as we hit the bush he would take over at the wheel. He had the eyes, and because he could spot everything, it was always an interesting trek in.

As soon as we reached the campsite, where we would launch the boat and start setting the traps, Steve was into it immediately. He would scan up and down the river system for an hour and a half, dozens of miles, getting to know where the crocs hung out. He was able to match a croc to each slide, each track, belly print, and foot mark in the mud. He even remembered crocodiles from the year before, recalling them by name.

As he set the traps, Steve specifically targeted different-sized animals that he and the other scientists had agreed to catch: big males, breeding females, and subadults. He set floating traps and soft mesh traps. Steve would often catch more crocs in a single day than the team could cope with.

Some of the crocodiles had amazing injuries. One had been hit by a crossbow. The arrow had stuck into the back of its head so deep that no probe that we used could find the end of the wound.

Other crocs had fought among themselves. One that we affectionately named Trevor had two broken legs. When we tried to pick up his front legs to tuck them into his sides, we felt only floppy bits of busted-up bone, which would twist in unnatural angles.

"I want to take this crocodile home," I said.

Steve laughed. "This croc is still big and fat and fighting fit," he said. "Don't worry about him."

As luck would have it, we caught Trevor a second time. "Here's the deal," I said to Steve. "If we catch this crocodile once more, I'm taking him home." He could see I was serious. Perhaps it was intentional that Steve never caught Trevor again.

We trapped several smaller females, all

around the nine-foot mark. That's when Steve stepped back and let the all-girl team take over: all the women in camp, zoo workers mainly, myself, and others. We would jump on the croc, help secure the tracking device, and let her go.

At one point Steve trapped a female that he could see was small and quiet. He turned to Bindi. "How would you like to jump the head?"

Bindi's eyes lit up. This was what she had been waiting for. Once Steve removed the croc from the trap and secured its jaws, the next step was for the point person to jump the croc's head. Everybody else on the team followed immediately afterward, pinning the crocodile's body.

"Don't worry," I said to Bindi. "I'll back you up." Or maybe I was really talking to Steve. He was nervous as he slipped the croc out of its mesh trap. He hovered over the whole operation, knowing that if anything went amiss, he was right there to help.

"Ready, and now!" he said. Bindi flung herself on the head of the crocodile. I came in right over her back. The rest of the girls jumped on immediately, and we had our croc secured.

"Let's take a photo with the whole family," Professor Franklin said. Bindi sat proudly at the crocodile's head, her hand casually draped over its eyes. Steve was in the middle, holding up the croc's front legs. Next in line was me. Finally, Robert had the tail. This shot ended up being our 2006 family Christmas card.

I look at it now and it makes me laugh out loud. The family that catches crocs together, rocks together. The Irwin family motto.

Steve, Bindi, and I are all smiling. But then there is Robert's oh-so-serious face. He has a top-jaw rope wrapped around his body, with knots throughout. He took his job seriously. He had the rope and was ready as the backup. He was on that croc's tail. It was all about catching crocs safely, mate. No mucking around here.

As we idled back in to camp, Robert said, "Can I please drive the boat?"

"Crikey, mate, you are two years old," Steve said. "I'll let you drive the boat next year."

But then, quite suddenly and without a word, Steve scooped Robert up and sat him up next to the outboard. He put the tiller in his hand.

"Here's what you do, mate," Steve said, and he began to explain how to drive the boat. He seemed in a hurry to impart as much wisdom to his son as possible.

Robert spent the trip jumping croc tails, driving the boat, and tying knots. Steve created a croc made of sticks and set it on a sandbar. He pulled the boat up next to it, and he, Robert, and Bindi went through all the motions of jumping the stick-croc.

"I'm going to say two words," Robert shouted, imitating his father. "'Go,' and 'Now.' First team off on 'Go,' second team off on 'Now.'" Then he'd yell "Go, now" at the top of his lungs. He and Steve jumped up as if the stick-croc was about to swing around and tear their arms off.

"Another croc successfully caught, mate," Steve said proudly. Robert beamed with pride too.

When he got back to *Croc One,* Robert wrangled his big plush crocodile toy. I listened, incredulous, as my not-yet-three-year-old son muttered the commands of a seasoned croc catcher. He had all the lingo down, verbatim.

"Get me a twelve-millimeter rope," Robert commanded. "I need a second one. Get that top-jaw rope under that tooth, yep, the eye tooth, get it secured. We'll need a third top-jaw rope for this one. Who's got a six-millimeter rope? Hand me my Leatherman. Cut that rope here. Get that satellite tracker on."

The stuffed animal thoroughly secured, Robert made as if to brush off his little hands. "Professor Franklin," he announced in his best grown-up voice, "it's your croc."

Watching Steve around the camp was witnessing a man at one with his environment. Steve had spent all his life perfecting his bush skills, first learning them at his father's side when he was a boy. He hero-worshiped Bob and finally became like his dad and then some.

Steve took all the knowledge he'd acquired over the years and added his own experience. Nothing seemed to daunt him, from green ants, mozzies, sand flies, and leeches, to constant wet weather. On Cape York we faced the obvious wildlife hazards, including feral pigs, venomous snakes, and huge crocodiles. I never saw Steve afraid of anything, except the chance of harm coming to someone he loved.

He learned how to take care of himself over the years he spent alone in the bush. But as his life took a sharp turn, into the unknown territory of celebrity-naturalist, he suddenly found himself with a whole film crew to watch out for.

Filming wildlife documentaries couldn't have happened without John Stainton, our producer. Steve always referred to John as the genius behind the camera, and that was true. The music orchestration, the editing, the knowledge of what would make good television and what wouldn't—these were all areas of John's clear expertise.

But on the ground, under the water, or in the bush, while we were actually filming, it was 100 percent Steve. He took care of the crew and eventually his family as well, while filming in some of the most remote, inaccessible, and dangerous areas on earth.

Steve kept the cameraman alive by telling him exactly when to shoot and when to run. He orchestrated what to film and where to film, and then located the wildlife. Steve's first rule, which he repeated to the crew over and over, was a simple one: *Film everything, no matter what happens.*

"If something goes wrong," he told the

crew, "you are not going to be of any use to me lugging a camera and waving your other arm around trying to help. Just keep rolling. Whatever the sticky situation is, I will get out of it."

Just keep rolling. Steve's mantra.

On all of our documentary trips, Steve packed the food, set up camp, fed the crew. He knew to take the extra tires, the extra fuel, the water, the gear. He anticipated the needs of six adults and two kids on every film shoot we ever went on.

As I watched him at Lakefield, the situation was no different. Our croc crews came and went, and the park rangers came and went, and Steve wound up organizing anywhere from twenty to thirty people.

Everyone did their part to help. But the first night, I watched while one of the crew put up tarps to cover the kitchen area. After a day or two, the tarps slipped, the ropes came undone, and water poured off into our camp kitchen.

After a full day of croc capture, Steve came back into camp that evening. He made no big deal about it. He saw what was going on. I watched him wordlessly shimmy up a tree, retie the knots, and resecure the tarps. What was once a collection of saggy, baggy tarps had been transformed into a well-secured roof.

Steve had the smooth and steady movements of someone who was self-assured after years of practice. He'd get into the boat, fire up the engine, and start immediately. There was never any hesitation. His physical strength was unsurpassed. He could chop wood, gather water, and build many things with an ease that was awkwardly obvious when anybody else (myself, for example) tried to struggle with the same task.

But when I think of all his bush skills, I treasured most his way of delivering up the natural world. On that croc research trip in the winter of 2006, Steve presented me with a series of memories more valuable than any piece of jewelry.

Every morning and evening at Lakefield, the fruit bats would come and go from the trees near our campsite. During the day, you could hear them in the distance as they squabbled over territory. Each fruit bat wanted to jockey for the best position on a branch. But when evening came, as if by silent agreement, all the bats knew to fly off at the same time.

Steve grabbed me and the kids one evening just at dusk, and we went out onto the river to watch the bats. I would rank that night as one of the most incredible experiences of my life, right up there with catching crocs and swimming with manatees.

Sitting at dusk with the kids in the boat, all of a sudden the trees came alive. The bats took flight, skimming over the water to delicately dip for a drink, flying directly over our heads. It was as if we had gone back in time and pterodactyls flew once again.

It was such an awe-inspiring event that we all fell quiet, the children included. The water was absolutely still, like an inky mirror, almost like oil. Not a single fish jumped, not a croc moved. All we heard were the wings of these ancient mammals in the darkening sky.

We lay quietly in the bottom of the boat, floating in the middle of this paradise. We knew that we were completely and totally safe. We were in a small dinghy in the middle of some of the most prolifically populated crocodile water, yet we were absolutely comfortable knowing that Steve was there with us.

"One day, babe," Steve said softly to me, "we'll look back on wildlife harvesting projects and things like croc farming the same way we look back on slavery and cannibalism. It will be simply an unbelievable part of human history. We'll get so beyond it that it will be something we will never, ever return to."

"We aren't there yet," I said.

He sighed. "No, we aren't."

I thought of the sign Steve had over his desk back home. It bore the word "warrior" and its definition: "One who is engaged in battle."

And it was a battle. It was a battle to protect fragile ecosystems like Lakefield from the wildlife perpetrators, from people who sought to kill anything that could turn a profit. These same people were out collecting croc eggs and safari-hunting crocodiles. They were working to legalize a whole host of illicit and destructive activities. They were lobbying to farm or export everything that moved, from these beautiful fruit bats we were watching, to magpie geese, turtles, and even whales.

That trip was epic. Every day was an adventure. Bindi sat down for her formal schooling at a little table under the big trees by the river, with the kookaburras singing and the occasional lizard or snake cruising through camp. She had the best scientists from the University of Queensland around to answer her questions.

I could tell Steve didn't want it to end. We had been in bush camp for five weeks. Bindi, Robert, and I were now scheduled for a trip to Tasmania. Along with us would be their teacher, Emma (the kids called her "Miss Emma"), and Kate, her sister, who also worked at the zoo. It was a trip I had planned for a long time. Emma would celebrate her thirtieth birthday, and Kate would see her first snow.

Steve and I would go our separate ways. He would leave Lakefield on *Croc One* and go directly to rendezvous with Philippe Cousteau for the filming of *Ocean's Deadliest*. We tried to figure out how we could all be together for the shoot, but there just wasn't enough room on the boat.

Still, Steve came to me one morning while I was dressing Robert. "Why don't you stay for two more days?" he said. "We could change your flight out. It would be worth it."

When I first met Steve, I made a deal with myself. Whenever Steve suggested a trip, activity, or project, I would go for it. I found it all too easy to come up with an excuse not to do something. "Oh, gee, Steve, I don't feel like climbing that mountain, or fording that river," I could have said. "I'm a bit tired, and it's a bit cold, or it's a bit hot and I'm a bit warm."

There always could be some reason. Instead I decided to be game for whatever Steve proposed. Inevitably, I found myself on the best adventures of my life.

For some reason, this time I didn't say yes. I fell silent. I thought about how it would work and the logistics of it all. A thousand concerns flitted through my mind. While I was mulling it over, I realized Steve had already walked off.

It was the first time I hadn't said, "Yeah, great, let's go for it." And I didn't really know why.

Steve drove us to the airstrip at the ranger station. One of the young rangers there immediately began to bend his ear about a wildlife issue. I took Robert off to pee on a bush before we had to get on the plane. It was just a tiny little prop plane and there would be no restroom until we got to Cairns.

When we came back, all the general talk meant that there wasn't much time left for us to say good-bye. Bindi pressed a note into Steve's hand and said, "Don't read this until we're gone." I gave Steve a big hug and a kiss. Then I kissed him again.

I wanted to warn him to be careful about diving. It was my same old fear and discomfort with all his underwater adventures. A few days earlier, as Steve stepped off a dinghy, his boot had gotten tangled in a rope.

"Watch out for that rope," I said.

He shot me a look that said, *I've just caught forty-nine crocodiles in three weeks, and you're thinking I'm going to fall over a rope?*

I laughed sheepishly. It seemed absurd to caution Steve about being careful.

Steve was his usual enthusiastic self as we climbed into the plane. We knew we would see each other in less than two weeks. I would head back to the zoo, get some work done, and leave for Tasmania.

Steve would do his filming trip. Then we would all be together again.

We had arrived at a remarkable place in our relationship. Our trip to Lakefield had been one of the most special months of my entire life. The kids had a great time. We were all in the same place together, not only physically, but emotionally, mentally, and spiritually.

We were all there.

The pilot fired up the plane. Robert had a seat belt on and couldn't see out the window. I couldn't lift him up without unbuckling him, so he wasn't able to see his daddy waving good-bye. But Bindi had a clear view of Steve, who had parked his Ute just outside the gable markers and was standing on top of it, legs wide apart, a big smile on his face, waving his hands over his head.

I could see Bindi's note in one of his hands. He had read it and was acknowledging it to Bindi. She waved frantically out the window. As the plane picked up speed, we swept past him and then we were into the sky.

CHAPTER EIGHTEEN

Batt Reef

It was a beautiful spring morning in September when I started packing for my trip. I was always excited to be heading for Tasmania, because it has got to be one of the most beautiful places on the face of the earth. There were five of us: the children, Kate, Emma, and myself.

The journey down meant a stopover in Melbourne, then a bumpy, turbulent ride over to Tasmania. Between the tip of South America and Tasmania, there's nothing except clear blue ocean, so the weather gets up a lot of steam. The infamous Roaring Forties winds crash through on the western side of the island state. I looked down from our small plane and saw some of the waves that Steve loved.

About two hundred miles off Tasmania's western shore is Shipstern's Bluff, with some of the biggest and best surf in the world. This is "big-wave" surfing, where the surfers have to be towed in, and it is not unusual to have sixty-foot faces on the waves.

Probably only around 5 percent of the surfers in the world would dare to even approach Shipstern's Bluff. As our plane made its approach, I saw sets of ragged, white-topped waves heading toward shore. I myself was not much of a water person, but I really enjoyed photographing or filming Steve in action.

We'll have to come back, I thought. *Steve and Bindi could surf here together now.*

But this trip was all about Tasmanian devils and snow. We were heading for Cradle Mountain to show Kate her first snow. The Sunshine Coast never gets any of the white stuff, so there are quite a few people there without firsthand experience of it. On the way to the mountain, we would stop at a beautiful little wildlife park near Launceston.

The park did its part by taking in orphaned Tasmanian devils. The mothers had died from the facial tumor disease ravaging the island's devil population. The park's goal was to determine whether the mothers had communicated the disease to the next generation. This trip would be to see the offspring of the babies who had survived.

We landed in Launceston, and I felt as though we were embarking on a great adventure, showing my friends the beautiful Tasmanian countryside. We had rented a pair of small cottages. It was cold, but the air was clean and fresh. Bindi, Robert, and I snuggled down in one cottage, while Emma and Kate had their own cottage nearby.

The next day was Sunday. In Australia we celebrate Father's Day in September, so it was natural for us to try and get in touch with Steve. I knew he was filming somewhere off the Queensland coast.

On board *Croc One,* along with Steve and Philippe Cousteau, was a toxicologist named Jamie Seymour. They planned to study several species of dangerous sea creatures, with the double goal of understanding their place in the environment and teaching people how to frequent Australia's waters more safely.

We tried to get through to Steve on the phone, but of course he was out filming. I spoke via satellite phone to another Kate, Kate Coulter, a longtime zoo employee, with her husband, Brian. We all took turns talking to her.

"Steve captured a huge sea snake," Kate said. "He said it was the biggest he had ever seen. He said, 'Thick as my arm, no, thick as my leg.' "

Kate knew Steve well, and she conveyed his enthusiasm perfectly. She told us she would pass along our messages.

"Tell Daddy how much I love him and miss him," Bindi said, and Kate told her she would. Robert wanted immediately to go see the big sea snake his father had caught. He didn't quite grasp that the Cape was thousands of miles away.

At the Launceston wildlife park, we met the new generation of baby devils. They were tiny, smaller than guinea pigs, and just starting to emerge from their mothers' pouches. Their mothers had been lucky to survive DFTD. An entire generation of devils could have been wiped out.

The park reminded me of our own Australia Zoo when it first started out. It was a family operation run by Dick and Judi Warren. They were both warm and friendly and eager to talk. Judi made us toasted sandwiches and hot drinks, while Dick told stories of satirizing the Baby Bob incident.

"I dressed up like Steve in a blond wig," Dick said. "Then I took a little baby doll in with the devils and fed them while holding this little doll."

He checked to make sure I was laughing, and I was. "It ended up on video on one of the ferries here on the island!" Judi said. Australians enjoy laughing at themselves and paying out on others. I've always found it refreshing.

We toured the park, seeing parrots, wombats, and tiger snakes. "Koalas and primates," Dick said. "We'll get some koalas and primates and then we'll be set."

I thought back to how many times Steve and I had said something similar. "Just one more species and then our zoo will be done." I was coming to realize that Australia Zoo would never be done. There were too many species in the world that needed our help.

Steve had tried to reach us after our Father's Day phone call. There was no way I could have realized that, because I didn't have any mobile phone reception at the cottage. He was back on *Croc One* and trying to get hold of us via satellite phone. I didn't know. I wouldn't be in range again until the next day. We enjoyed our dinner, built a huge fire, and snuggled down for the night.

We didn't hurry ourselves the next day. We meandered west, stopping at a raspberry farm and at the Honey Factory in Chudleigh. They featured a beehive behind glass, and we loved watching as the bees worked on their honeycomb. They never stopped to say, "I wonder what the meaning of life is." They just kept building.

The Honey Factory also featured a plethora of bee-themed products: bee gum boots, bee back massagers, bee umbrellas, and a bee trolley for the kids to ride on. Bindi sampled every single flavor of honey that they had. She bought a wristwatch with a bee on it. Robert picked out a backpack.

"Robert," I said, "that backpack is great. It has bees on it."

"It has one bee on it," he said, correcting me.

"Oh, okay, one bee," I said, amused at my son's seriousness.

We spent the last hour of the morning at the Honey Factory. As we walked out the door, Bindi looked at her newly purchased watch and said, "It's twelve o'clock." We all stopped for a moment and considered that it was twelve o'clock. Then we got into the car and left.

Our destination that day was Cradle Mountain National Park. We were still not in mobile phone range, so I planned to check in when we reached the resort, where we had rented rooms. We wanted to hike the mountain to the snowline.

We drove into the Cradle Mountain resort still munching on raspberries. Emma and Kate waited with the kids in the car.

"I'll just be a minute," I said. "I'll check in and we'll head to our rooms." The currawongs were calling, and a padymelon, a small version of a roo, hopped off a wall just at the edge of the car park as I went in.

"Where's all the snow?" I asked the woman behind the desk.

"It snowed this morning," she said.

"Well, good," I said. "There's hope."

Then she passed me a note. She said, "Frank called from the zoo."

"I'm not surprised," I said. "I haven't called the zoo all day, and Frank is always trying to track me down."

"Why don't you come take the call in the office?" she said. I thought that was a little odd, since when I had been there before I'd always used the pay phone near the pub at the resort. But I entered the office and sat down in a big, comfortable chair. I could see the car park out the window. Emma and Kate were still out at the car. Robert had fallen asleep, and Kate sat inside with him. Bindi smiled and laughed with Emma.

"How you going, Frank?" I said into the phone.

He said, "Hi, Terri. I've been trying to get hold of you for a while." His voice had a heavy, serious tone.

"Well, I've just got here," I said. "Sorry about that, but I'm here now. What's up?"

"I'm sorry to say that Steve had a bit of an accident while he was diving," Frank said. "I'm afraid he got hit in the chest by a stingray's barb."

I'm sure there wasn't much of a pause, but I felt time stop. I knew what Frank was going to say next. I just kept repeating the same thing over and over in my head.

Don't say it, don't say it, don't say it.

Then Frank said the three words I did not want him to say. "And he died."

I took a deep breath and looked out the window. There was Bindi, so happy to have finally arrived at one of her favorite places. We were going to have fun. She had brought her teacher and Kate. She was so excited. And the world stopped. I took another breath.

"Thank you very much for calling, Frank," I said. I didn't know what I was saying. I was overwhelmed, already on autopilot. "You need to cancel the rest of our trip, you need to contact my family in Oregon, and you need to get us home."

So it began.

I knew the one thing I wanted to do more than anything was to get to Steve. I needed to bring my kids home as fast as possible. I didn't understand what had been going on in the rest of the world. Steve's accident had occurred at eleven o'clock in the morning. The official time of death was made at twelve noon, the exact time that Bindi had looked at her watch and said, for no apparent reason, "It's twelve o'clock."

Now I had to go out to the car and tell Bindi and Robert what had happened to their daddy. How do you tell an eight-year-old child that her father has died? A two-year-old boy?

The person they loved most in the world was gone, the person they looked up to, relied on, and emulated, who played with them in the bubble bath and told them stories about when he was a naughty little boy, who took them for motorbike rides and got them ice cream, went on croc-catching adventures and showed them the world's wildlife.

I had to tell them that they had lost this most important person, on this most beautiful day.

Emma came in and I told her what had happened. Suddenly I felt very sick. I didn't know if I could stand up, and I asked to use the restroom. Then I realized this was the exact time for me to be strong. For years I had counted on Steve's strength. At six feet tall and two hundred pounds, he was a force to be reckoned with. But he always told me there were different kinds of strength. Steve said he could count on me to be strong when times were hard.

I thought about that, and I suddenly understood there must be a reason that I was here and he was gone. I needed to help his kids, to be there for our children. All I wanted to do was run, and run, and run. But I had to stay.

With Emma at my side, I went outside and climbed into the car. Bindi had opened up the raspberries again. I put them away and sat her down. She knew instantly by my face that something was wrong.

"Did something happen to one of the animals at the zoo?" she asked.

"Something happened to Daddy," I said. "He was diving, and he had an accident." I told her everything that I knew about what had happened. She cried. We all cried. Robert still slept.

It was back and forth, in and out of the resort now, making phone call after phone call. The challenge was getting home. I couldn't comprehend the massive response by the press—we were being tracked down like prey, the helicopters already hovering in the air. Taking a commercial flight home was out of the question, so we managed to find a charter plane.

"We can drive," Emma said gently to me, meaning herself and Kate. We had to get to the airport and run the gauntlet of the media. I suddenly felt a real desire to take charge, to be in control and not to fall in a heap. I knew I needed to be strong.

"I can drive," I said.

It was on an impossibly narrow, winding section of road that Robert decided to wake up. So I had to drive and at the same time tell my son what had happened.

"Where's Cradle Mountain?" he asked.

"We had to leave Cradle Mountain, Robert," I said. Then I explained to him that his father had had an accident. He asked me to explain everything again, and I did for a second time.

Robert stopped talking. He held on to Piggy, his little plush friend. He feverishly worked Piggy's ears through his fingers, staring out the window. For a half hour he didn't say a word.

When we got close to the airport, the reality of the public reaction to Steve's death began to sink in. Members of the media were everywhere. We drove straight through the gates to pull up right next to the charter plane. The last thing I felt like doing at that moment was to talk to anyone about what had happened. I just wanted to get to Steve.

As I walked toward the plane, I turned

back to thank the police who had helped us. The tears in their eyes shocked me out of my own personal cocoon of grief. This wasn't just a job for them. They genuinely felt for us, and suffered Steve's loss. *So many other people loved him too,* I thought.

All during the endless, three-hour plane ride to Maroochydore, I kept flashing back to our fourteen years of adventures together. My mind kept focusing on another plane ride, so similar to this one, when Bindi and I had to fly from the United States back to Australia after Steve's mum had died. Part of me wished we could have flown forever, never landing, never facing what we were about to. I concentrated on Bindi and Robert, getting them fed and making sure they were comfortable. But the thought of that last sad flight stayed there in the back of my mind.

The plane landed at Maroochydore in the dark. We taxied in between hangars, out of public view. I think it was raining, but perhaps it wasn't, maybe I was just sad. As I came down the steps of the plane, Frank, Joy, and Wes stood there. We all hugged one another. Wes sobbed. We managed to help one another to the hangar, where we all piled into two vehicles for the half-hour drive back to the zoo.

I turned on the DVD in the backseat for the kids. I desperately needed a moment without having to explain what was going on. I wanted to talk to Wes, Joy, and Frank. At some point during the ride, Wes reached back and closed the DVD player. The light from the player was giving the press the opportunity to film and photograph us in the car.

This was a time to be private and on our own. *How clever of Wes to consider that,* I thought, right in the middle of everything.

"Wes," I said, "what are we going to do now?"

CHAPTER NINETEEN

Steve's Whale One

In October of 1991, on the day I met Steve, it was only by chance that I stopped at his wildlife park at all. I had been sleeping in the backseat of a car on the way back from a barbecue at a friend of a friend's house. Up front, Lori's friend knew I was interested in zoos. When he saw a sign for this one, he debated with himself whether he should wake me. Even when he did, I wasn't sure if this reptile park was going to be much more than a few snakes in little glass tanks.

So it was only by chance that I was on that highway at all, and only chance that I stopped. And it was only by chance that Steve conducted the croc show that day. Some days, Wes did the show.

Chance. Fate. Destiny.

These were words I lived by. I believed my life had been shaped for a special purpose. But with Steve's death my faith was tested. Was it pure chance that Steve, a man who cheated mortality almost every single day of his adult life, died in such a bizarre accident?

During the decade and a half that I knew him, I don't think a week went by when he didn't get a bite, blow, or injury of some kind. His knee and shoulder plagued him from years of jumping crocs. As Steve erected a fence at our Brigalow Belt conservation property, a big fence-post driver he was using slipped and landed directly on his head, compressing the fifth disk in his neck. Even injured, he still managed to push on—at the zoo, filming, and doing heavy construction. He went at work like a bull at a gate. He climbed trees with orangutans. He traversed the most remote deserts and the most impossible mountains. He packed his life chock-a-block full with risks of all kinds.

"I get called an adrenaline junkie every other minute," Steve said. "I'm just fine with that."

One crowded hour of glorious life is worth more than an age without a name. I had no regrets for Steve's glorious life, and I know he couldn't have lived any other way.

When Bindi, Robert, and I got home on the evening of Steve's death, we encountered a strange scene that we ourselves had created. The plan had been that Steve would get back from his *Ocean's Deadliest* film shoot before we got back from Tasmania. So we'd left the house with a funny surprise for him.

We got large plush toys and arranged them in a grouping to look like the family. We sat one that represented me on the sofa, a teddy bear about her size for Bindi, and a plush orangutan for Robert. We dressed the smaller toys in the kids' clothes, and the big doll in my clothes. I went to the zoo photographer and got close-up photographs of our faces that we taped onto the heads of the dolls. We posed them as if we were having dinner, and I wrote a note for Steve.

"Surprise," the note said. "We didn't go to Tasmania! We are here waiting for you and we love you and miss you so much! We will see you soon. Love, Terri, Bindi, and Robert."

The surprise was meant for Steve when he returned and we weren't there. Instead the dolls silently waited for us, our plush-toy doubles, ghostly reminders of a happier life.

Wes, Joy, and Frank came into the house with me and the kids. We never entertained, we never had anyone over, and now suddenly our living room seemed full. Unaccustomed to company, Robert greeted each one at the door.

"Take your shoes off before you come in," he said seriously. I looked over at him. He was clearly bewildered but trying so hard to be a little man.

We had to make arrangements to bring Steve home. I tried to keep things as private as possible. One of Steve's former classmates at school ran the funeral home in Caloundra that would be handling the arrangements. He had known the Irwin family for years, and I recall thinking how hard this was going to be for him as well.

Bindi approached me. "I want to say good-bye to Daddy," she said.

"You are welcome to, honey," I said. "But you need to remember when Daddy said good-bye to his mother, that last image of her haunted him while he was awake and asleep for the rest of his life."

I suggested that perhaps Bindi would like

to remember her daddy as she last saw him, standing on top of the truck next to that outback airstrip, waving good-bye with both arms and holding the note that she had given him. Bindi agreed, and I knew it was the right decision, a small step in the right direction.

I knew the one thing that I had wanted to do all along was to get to Steve. I felt an urgency to continue on from the zoo and travel up to the Cape to be with him. But I knew what Steve would have said. His concern would have been getting the kids settled and in bed, not getting all tangled up in the media turmoil.

Our guests decided on their own to get going and let us get on with our night. I gave the kids a bath and fixed them something to eat. I got Robert settled in bed and stayed with him until he fell asleep. Bindi looked worried. Usually I curled up with Robert in the evening, while Steve curled up with Bindi. "Don't worry," I said to her. "Robert's already asleep. You can sleep in my bed with me."

Little Bindi soon dropped off to sleep, but I lay awake. It felt as though I had died and was starting over with a new life. I mentally reviewed my years as a child growing up in Oregon, as an adult running my own business, then meeting Steve, becoming his wife and the mother of our children. Now, at age forty-two, I was starting again.

I kept going over and over what had happened. I wanted to talk to everyone who had been there with Steve on the day of his accident. But I thought it more important to focus on our life together instead. Often, while we were on an adventure, it struck me as almost surreal for us to be in a tropical rain forest, for example, or on a South Pacific island, visiting the Galapagos, or trekking in snow-capped wilderness in America. I felt like I had been living in a movie.

I lay there while the clock ticked on. *Here is another minute I have survived without Steve.* I consoled myself with the thought that the clock was ticking for all of us. None of us could know when it was going to be our time. I resolved that I would celebrate the people who were still here and apply myself to the work that still had to be done. My resolution was all well and good, but what really sustained me during those dark, lonely hours of the night was another deeper, more persistent thought. With every tick of the clock, I was one moment closer to being with Steve again. As strong as Steve was in this life, I knew without a doubt he would be a force to be reckoned with in the next.

The first morning was especially hard. Usually our morning routine involved listening with one ear for the sound of a motorbike approaching the house. Steve never slept more than a few hours a night. He was always up before us and would go about his zoo business and then come back, riding up to the house and bursting through the door. He'd wrestle the kids and tell them about something new and exciting going on in the zoo, and then he would bundle them up, with me protesting that they needed hats or coats, or hadn't brushed their teeth—and no matter what I said, he would spirit them off out the door and onto the motorbike.

That first morning, the realization sank in that he wasn't going to come bursting in anymore.

Using the satellite phone connection, I finally reached *Croc One*. The captain, Kris, was in tears. I finally tracked down John

Stainton, and he assured me that he hadn't left Steve's side.

"I've got a charter plane coming," John said. "I'll get him home, Terri."

I asked about Steve's personal effects. Steve had had on his khakis and wet-suit boots while he was diving, but because he had no jewelry or anything of value, the medical examiner had destroyed all his clothing.

I was devastated. It's completely unpredictable what one will hold dear in a time of grief, particularly in the case of an accident. I remember thinking, *I've got to sit down with the powers that be and change these regulations.* The family should decide what should be destroyed and what should be kept. I needed to focus on something other than losing Steve. That fact was just too hard to get my head around.

As John arranged to bring Steve home, the media pressure steadily increased. I told Wes I wanted to go meet the plane, but that I wouldn't take the kids. This was my time to be with my soul mate, and I needed to do it on my own. I headed out with a police escort. The Queensland police were considerate and professional, and an officer named

Annie was personally assigned to make sure the overwhelming media attention did not interfere with my private moment to say good-bye to Steve.

Wes accompanied me. It was night. As the seaplane came in, I recognized it as the same one that had taken Steve on many South Pacific adventures, in search of sea snakes, crested iguanas, or sharks. The ranks of police stood at attention. Many of them had met Steve previously. Once again, I was overwhelmed to see the looks of grief on their faces.

The plane landed, and I had a moment to sit with Steve on my own. It was a bit of an effort to clamber up into the back of the plane. A simple wooden casket rested inside, still secured. I knew that who Steve was, his spirit and his soul, were no longer there, but it was strange how I couldn't cry.

I sat down and leaned my head against the wooden box that held his body and felt such strange peace.

In some way, we were together again.

As I write this, I am still waiting for Steve to walk through the door. His sarong still hangs on the bed. His toothbrush is in the bathroom.

Reality is sinking in more and more. Bindi and I have a lot of heart-to-heart talks. These seem to help her, just like when she was younger and lost a special koala named Wilson. Wilson died of renal failure and is buried in our backyard. I felt thankful that over the years, I had set the foundation of faith with Bindi.

"As hard as it is to understand, there was a reason for all of this," I told her. "One day it will be clear."

Robert is like a pitiful puppy, and he still waits patiently for his daddy to come home from heaven. I hadn't been prepared for how devastated Robert would be. Some nights he sits in the bathtub and cries. "I want my daddy," he says, over and over. It absolutely tears my heart out.

We have a dear friend, a wonderful psychologist who has helped a great deal—he suffered a loss in his own family recently, and we both felt sad. He explained that grief is your own process. You can't compare your grief to anyone else's. It is something that is uniquely yours. People outside our immediate circle murmured concern that perhaps Bindi was coping a little too well with her grief, and I wasn't immune to comments in the press about her remarkably composed speech at Steve's memorial service. It was nice to have my friend's professional opinion to put my mind at ease.

"That's what you are aiming for," he told me. "You are trying to raise children who can cope with life and not fall apart. That's the goal. Understanding that where there is love there is grief, and where there is life there is death, and that a person's spirit and soul never die and that their love never ends—these are important lessons to impart to our children."

Bindi does do well. It will take more time with Robert. I learned that as Bindi gets older and reaches adolescence, there may be another period when grief revisits her. Knowing that, I can prepare her for the rough patches ahead.

Because of the constant media surveillance, I could not venture out to see the countless tributes that mourners laid down in front of the zoo. But all the items were collected and stored safely, and we now display a lovely memorial selection.

The public response to Steve's death

would have overwhelmed him most of all—the kind thoughts, prayers, sympathy, and tears. I wasn't facing this grief on my own. So many people from around the world were trying to come to terms with it as well. The process seemed particularly difficult for children who had not had the opportunity to experience the circle of life as Bindi had. I felt it was important to get a message out to them. When your hero dies, everything he stood for does not end. Everything he stood for must continue.

There was never a doubt in my mind that I'd keep working toward stopping the destruction of our environment and wildlife that was spiraling out of control. There were so many triumphs that Steve had already worked so hard for.

I sat down with Wes. "First, we're going to work on everything Steve wanted to achieve," I said. "Then we'll move on to everything that we were collectively working toward. And finally, I want to continue with my own goals, in terms of our conservation work."

We strategized about the expansion of the zoo. I didn't want to just maintain the zoo as it was, I wanted to follow Steve's plans for the future. I felt that I was still having this wonderful, cheeky, competitive relationship with Steve.

Wes and I took the stacks of plans, blueprints, and manila folders from Steve's desk. I assembled them and laid them out on a conference table.

"This was Steve's plan for Australia Zoo over the next ten years," I said. "I want to do it in five."

We would secure more land. I remember the first two acres we ever bought to enlarge the zoo, how Steve and I sat with our arms around each other, looking at the property next door and dreaming. Now we were negotiating for an additional five hundred acres of forestry land. This tract would join the existing zoo property with the five hundred acres of our conservation property, bringing our total to fifteen hundred acres at Australia Zoo.

This winter we christened *Steve's Whale One,* a whale-watching excursion boat that will realize another of his long-held dreams. He always wanted to expand the experience of the zoo to include whales. *Steve's Whale One* is a way for people to see firsthand some of the most amazing creatures on earth. The humpbacks in Australian waters approach whale-watching boats with curiosity and openness. It is a delightful experience, and one that I am confident will work to help inspire people and end the inhumane practice of whaling.

Bindi the Jungle Girl aired on July 18, 2007, on ABC (Channel 2) in Australia, and we were so proud. Bindi's determination to carry on her father's legacy was a testament to everything Steve believed in. He had perfectly combined his love for his family with his love for conservation and leaving the world a better place. Now this love was perfectly passed down to his kids.

The official beginning of Bindi's career was a fantastic day. All the time and effort, and joy and sorrow of the past year culminated in this wonderful series. Now everyone was invited to see Bindi's journey, first filming with her dad, and then stepping up and filming with Robert and me. It was also a chance to experience one more time why Steve was so special and unique, to embrace him, to appreciate him, and to celebrate his life.

Bindi, Robert, and I would do our best to

make sure that Steve's light wasn't hidden under a bushel. It would continue to shine as we worked together to protect all wildlife and all wild places.

After Bindi's show launched, it seemed so appropriate that another project we had been working on for many months came to fruition. We found an area of 320,000 acres in Cape York Peninsula, bordered on one side by the Dulcie River and on the other side by the Wenlock River—some of the best crocodile country in the world. It was one of the top spots in Australia, and the most critically important habitat in the state of Queensland. Prime Minister John Howard, along with the Queensland government, dedicated $6.3 million to obtaining this land, in memory of Steve.

On July 22, 2007, the Steve Irwin Wildlife Reserve became official. This piece of land means so much to the Irwin family, and I know what it would have meant to Steve. Ultimately, it meant the protection of his crocodiles, the animals he loved so much.

What does the future hold for the Irwin family? Each and every day is filled with incredible triumphs and moments of terrible grief. And in between, life goes on. We are determined to continue to honor and appreciate Steve's wonderful spirit. It lives on with all of us. Steve lived every day of his life doing what he loved, and he always said he would die defending wildlife. I reckon Bindi, Robert, and I will all do the same.

God bless you, Stevo. I love you, mate.

Come Join Us

Come join us in the effort to save the world's wildlife. You can find Wildlife Warriors on the Web at www.wildlifewarriors.org, or write to either of these addresses:

Wildlife Warriors Worldwide,
World Headquarters
P.O. Box 29, Beerwah,
Queensland 4519, Australia

Or:

Wildlife Warriors Worldwide USA
P.O. Box 11347
Eugene, OR 97400, USA

And remember, crocs rule!

Condolence

After Steve's death I received letters of condolence from people all over the world. I would like to thank everyone who sent such thoughtful sympathy. Your kind words and support gave me the strength to write this book and so much more. Carolyn Male is one of those dear people who expressed her thoughts and feelings after we lost Steve. It was incredibly touching and special, and I wanted to express my appreciation and gratitude. I'm happy to share it with you.

It is with a still-heavy heart that I rise this evening to speak about the life and death of one of the greatest conservationists of our time: Steve Irwin. Many people describe

Steve Irwin as a larrikin, inspirational, spontaneous. For me, the best way I can describe Steve Irwin is formidable. He would stand and fight, and was not to be defeated when it came to looking after our environment. When he wanted to get things done—whether that meant his expansion plans for the zoo, providing aid for animals affected by the tsunami and the cyclones, organizing scientific research, or buying land to conserve its environmental and habitat values—he just did it, and woe betide anyone who stood in his way. I am not sure I have ever met anyone else who was so determined to get the conservation message out across the globe, and I believe he achieved his aim. What I admired most about him was that he lived the conservation message every day of his life.

Steve's parents, Bob and Lyn, passed on their love of the Australian bush and their passion for rescuing and rehabilitating wildlife. Steve took their passion and turned it into a worldwide crusade. The founding of Wildlife Warriors Worldwide in 2002 provided Steve and Terri with another vehicle to raise awareness of conservation by allowing individuals to become personally involved in protecting injured, threatened, or endangered wildlife. It also has generated a working fund that helps with the wildlife hospital on the zoo premises and supports work with endangered species in Asia and Africa.

Research was always high on Steve's agenda, and his work has enabled a far greater understanding of crocodile behavior, population, and movement patterns. Working with the Queensland Parks and Wildlife Service and the University of Queensland, Steve was an integral part of the world's first Crocs in Space research program. His work will live on and inform us for many, many years to come.

Our hearts go out to his family and the Australia Zoo family. It must be difficult to work at the zoo every day with his larger-than-life persona still very much evident. Everyone must still be waiting for him to walk through the gate. His presence is everywhere, and I hope it lives on in the hearts and minds of generations of wildlife warriors to come. We have lost a great man in Steve Irwin. It is a great loss to the conservation movement. My heart and the hearts of everyone here goes out to his family.

Carolyn Male, Member for Glass House, Queensland, Australia
October 11, 2006

Glossary of Australian Terms

back block: the sticks; the back forty; remote acreage
billabong: oxbow river, slough, or watering hole
billy lid: child
bloke: man, guy
bloody: very, an intensifier
Bob's your uncle: exclamation meaning "and you're done!"
bore: underground well
brolga: large, gray crane
bull bar: heavy bar fixed to the front of a vehicle
capsule: infant car seat
caravan: trailer
chock-a-block: completely full
chough: crowlike bird

coldie: can of beer
cooee: traditional Australian call of "halloo!"
crikey: expression of surprise; "Wow!"
cuppa: cup of tea
currawong: ravenlike bird
dag: goofy person
daks: trousers
dam: pool, pond, or water hole
Digger: Australian soldier
doco: documentary
dunny: lavatory
dunny roll: toilet paper
esky: ice chest; short for "Eskimo"
fair dinkum, dinkum: true; real; genuine
footy: football (rugby)
freshie: freshwater crocodile
g'day: hello
good on you: good for you; well done
jabiru: large stork
joey: baby kangaroo, wombat, koala, or other marsupial baby
larrikin: good-time guy; prankster
lolly: a candy or a sweet-flavored treat
mate: buddy; friend
mozzie: mosquito
muster: round up sheep or cattle
paying out: making fun; teasing

phascogale: insectivorous Australian marsupial
Queenslander: raised house that usually has a large veranda or porch
right, she'll be: it'll be all right
roo: kangaroo
rufous bettong: small marsupial that can hop like a kangaroo
saltie: saltwater crocodile
spotty: spotlight
stacks: loads; tons
swag: bedroll; sleeping bag
torch: flashlight
Ute: pickup truck
windscreen: windshield
yabby: freshwater crayfish

Acknowledgments

I would like to thank my children, Bindi and Robert, for patiently supporting me while I spent many evenings and weekends writing this book (or as Robert used to say, "Mum is doing her schoolwork.").

Thanks also to those who helped entertain, feed, bathe, and wrangle my kids while I wrote (it does take a village!): Barry and Shelley Lyon, Emma Schell, Jeanette Covacevich, John and Bonnie Marineau, Brian and Sherri Marineau, April Harvie, Brian and Kate Coulter, Thelma Engle.

A special thank-you to my dear friend John Edward. If it wasn't for you, this book would never have been written.

Thanks to my precious friends and family, who were my sounding boards: Wes Mannion, Frank and Joy Muscillo, John Stainton, Judi Bailey, Craig Franklin, Bob Irwin.

A huge thank-you to Kate Schell, who helped me assemble my first draft—there were 250,000 words of stories that made us laugh and cry. You took the journey with me.

I would also like to thank Gil Reavill, for taking nine hundred pages and helping me choose which stories to keep for the final draft. Natasha Stoynoff, you were ready to help as a collaborator. I hope we actually get to work together one day. And to Ursula Cary, thank you for flying all the way to Australia to help me catch crocs for research and make those final edits.

I'd like to extend a big thank-you to all the interesting people who helped to shape our lives and are included in the pages of this book.

And finally, a huge thank-you to my husband, Steve. You are now the angel leaning over my shoulder, whispering in my ear that I can do anything—you always believed in me.